The Pledge

One Nation Under God

The Pledge

One Nation Under God

William J. Murray

LIVING
INK
BOOKS
Writing Worth Reading

ISBN: 978-089957035-8

First printing—May 2007

Cover designed by Meyer's Design, Houston, Texas

Interior design and typesetting by Reider Publishing Services,
    West Hollywood, California

Edited and proofread by Rich Cairnes, Dan Penwell, Sharon Neal, and
    Rick Steele

Printed in Canada
13 12 11 10 09 08 07 –T– 8 7 6 5 4 3 2 1

Library of Congress Cataloging-in-Publication Data
Murray, William J. (William Joseph), 1946-
    The pledge : one nation under God / William J. Murray.
        p. cm.
    Summary: "The Pledge traces our religious freedoms to the settlement of America and asserts that the legal attacks against the "Pledge of Allegiance" are part of a nationwide, coordinated effort spearheaded by the ACLU and militant atheists like Michael Newdow to change America's culture and government into totally secularized, godless entities"--Provided by publisher.
    ISBN 978-0-89957-035-8 (pbk. : alk. paper)
    1. Freedom of religion--United States. 2. Church and state--United States. 3. Bellamy, Francis. Pledge of Allegiance to the Flag. I. Title.
    BR516.M87 2007
    323.44'20973--dc22
                                                                2007008658

This work is dedicated to the men and women of the Armed Services of the United States of America and their families who have paid the price of freedom with blood, sweat, and tears that this nation may remain "One Nation under God."

■ Contents

■ Foreword

THE individual many view as the founder of the Democratic Party, Thomas Jefferson, has these words engraved on his beautiful memorial in Washington, DC: "GOD WHO GAVE US LIFE GAVE US LIBERTY." These are Jefferson's own words, and the quotation goes on to say: "Can the liberties of a nation be secure when we have removed a conviction that these liberties are the gift of God?"

The author of our Declaration of Independence completely understood that it is impossible to assert that Americans have inalienable rights and at the same time ignore the Being who gave us those inalienable rights—God himself.

This concept goes to the heart of what America has always stood for and fought for: We believe there is a God who gives basic rights to all people, and that it is the job of government to protect those rights.

Recent court decisions have stated that American citizens cannot publicly acknowledge God. Pronouncements like this rip the heart out of the logic of what makes up America—that our rights come from God himself. And the judges who make such decisions thumb their nose at Thomas Jefferson, the Declaration of Independence, and our 300-plus years of history.

Today we have good reason to fear the Supreme Court that gave us the infamous *Kelo v. New London* decision—saying private property can be confiscated from individuals and redistributed to other citizens without a public purpose, thus totally ignoring the Fifth Amendment. And American citizens are reasonably concerned that the Supreme Court may also decide to take the First Amendment, turn it upside down, and use it as a sword of censorship rather than as a plow for the fertile ground of free speech.

Our founders guaranteed American citizens the freedom *of* religion as the first right under the First Amendment. Radicals, proclaiming themselves "progressives," now seek to enforce a policy of freedom *from* all contact with religion. These so-called progressives declare that lest anyone's sensibilities be slightly offended, no one should be confronted, even tangentially, with the history, the fact, or the practice of faith in the public square.

Unable to win elections because of the unpopularity of the progressive agenda, the ACLU and those who share their hostility toward religion resort to employing the brute force of their comrades on the court bench. An arrogant, overreaching judiciary now seeks to bend the American public to their will. Matters that would never be approved by popular vote are forced on a compliant citizenry. Cities and states give in to the coerced fear of paying not only for the legitimate defense of their heritage and their citizens' sentiments, but also of paying exorbitant legal fees triggered by lone malcontents.

When the citizens do rise to action, these "progressives" in black robes can be relied upon to thwart the will of the people. Irrespective of the vote margin, the courts, when asked to intervene on behalf of an ACLU client, reliably attack the majority's decision—and at the same time impugn the motives and intelligence of the voters. This judicial *tour de force* not only ignores the voice of the people, but also often denies the will of the public entirely. We have seen this arrogant judicial activism in several recent cases, among them:

Hamdan v. Rumsfeld, in which U.S. constitutional rights were extended to terrorists. In addition, Geneva convention rights were extended to cowards who hid behind women and children and used houses of worship and hospitals as sanctuaries from which to attack and kill American and Allied uniformed troops.

The various *Paulson v. City of San Diego* cases, in which judges have ordered the Memorial Cross in the Korean War Cemetery at Mount Soledad in San Diego, California, removed—although the property was transferred to the federal government to protect it from just such an order. The assaults go on unabated.

The *Kelo v. New London* decision, as noted previously, authorizes theft of private property by governmental bodies that may in turn give the property to private interests for profitable exploitation.

William J. Murray stands in the gap and spells out the strategies with which Americans can assert their rights against the bellicose forces of irreligion. He defines not only the problem, but also clearly declares the too-often-ignored reality of our nation's historical reliance upon God and our long history of public ceremonial acknowledgment of him. Bill fittingly calls the community of faith to action, to rise one more time in righteous defense of the foundational covenants of this great nation's belief in the idea that "GOD WHO GAVE US LIFE GAVE US LIBERTY."

President Abraham Lincoln well stated our need for a faithful adherence to the Constitution: "Our safety, our liberty, depends upon preserving the Constitution of the United States as our fathers made it inviolate. The people of the United States are the rightful masters of both Congress and the courts, not to overthrow the Constitution, but to overthrow the men who pervert the Constitution."

William J. Murray rightly exhorts us again to take up Mr. Lincoln's call.

U.S. Representative Todd Akin
Republican from Missouri

■ Preface
Pledge Protection Act:
Delay Is Not Defeat

*And for the support of this Declaration, with a firm reliance on
the protection of divine Providence, we mutually pledge to each
other our Lives, our Fortunes and our sacred Honor.*

—THE UNITED STATES DECLARATION OF
INDEPENDENCE FROM ENGLAND, JULY 4, 1776

I BEGAN writing this book in early 2006. At that time I
had high hopes of seeing passage of the Pledge Protection
Act in the House and Senate and fully expected it to be
signed into law before the midterm elections in November
2006.

In June 2006, the Religious Freedom Coalition (of which I
am founder) organized a large rally and news conference in a
park near the Capitol building. Both of the original sponsors of
this important bill, Senator Jon Kyl (R-AZ) and Representative
Todd Akin (R-MO), spoke at this event and urged passage of
this legislation. We had been promised that the Pledge Protection Act would pass on Flag Day, June 14. That failed to happen because of events described in this book.

Eventually, the House of Representatives did pass the Pledge Protection Act of 2005 on August 19, 2006, but social liberals in the Senate defeated it.

An American nightmare occurred on November 7, 2006, when a Democratic Party controlled by radical secularists such as San Francisco radical Nancy Pelosi gained control of both the House of Representatives and the Senate due to voter disgust with Republicans over a war gone badly in Iraq and numerous Republican scandals.

The social conservative cause lost many good men in the House and Senate on election night. One of the greatest pro-family, pro-life allies lost was Senator Rick Santorum (R-PA) who had been a stalwart in the battle to defend God, life, and country. He was the founder of the Congressional Working Group on Religious Freedom that under Democratic party rule no longer exists. Another great loss to the pro-family movement was the defeat of Representative John Hostettler of Indiana. He had introduced the Public Expression of Religion Act, which I mention in this book. Representative Jim Ryun, former Olympic runner and a great prayer warrior in the Congress, was also defeated.

In January 2007, when the reins of power went to Speaker Nancy Pelosi over half of the born-again Christian, conservative Catholic, and Jewish employees of committees lost their jobs to secularists. The party in control has roughly two employees on each committee for every one of the minority party.

The hard truth is that with social radicals such as John Conyers of Michigan and Ted Kennedy of Massachusetts chairing committees in both the House and Senate, it will be difficult if not impossible to pass the Pledge Protection Act or other social conservative legislation. Worse, many of the protections in existing legislation are in danger of being removed.

But I am not giving up hope. I believe that the defeats suffered are a wake-up call for caring social conservatives, both Christian and Jewish, to become more aggressive and determined to take back control of Congress from radical secularists such as Speaker Nancy Pelosi in the 2008 election. Better yet is the opportunity to elect Republicans who are true social conservatives and not the handpicked social liberals of big business whose only interest is lower taxes for the wealthy.

Many things will become worse under liberal control in the House and the Senate during the next two years. Our national security will suffer. We will lose the ability to have judicial conservatives appointed to the federal bench. And very little will be done to protect the unborn or defend religious freedom. The worse the situation for our nation gets with radicals running the Congress, the better the opportunity for social conservatives to have real victories in coming elections.

As bad as the defeat of the Republican Party was for social conservatives in 2006, the fact is that God still rules in the affairs of men—and he knows what the future will bring. He also knows that there are millions of courageous men and women in America who love their country and are willing to fight to defend the religious freedoms that the Founding Fathers so cherished.

Social conservatives who love freedom for all including the baby in the womb must educate and encourage Americans to learn about the true history of this great nation and get them involved in the political process. It is my prayer that this book will help educate you to action.

I am optimistic about the future. It is my hope that you will be blessed, informed, inspired, and energized by what you read regarding our wonderful nation and its heritage of religious freedom.

When the Founding Fathers signed the Declaration of Independence in 1776, they pledged their lives, their fortunes, and their sacred honor to defend religious and political liberty. We can do no less in the twenty-first century.

William J. Murray
Chairman
Religious Freedom Coalition

CHAPTER 1

America: One Nation Under God

> *In the name of God, Amen. We, whose names are underwritten,*
> *the loyal subjects of our dread Sovereign Lord King James, by*
> *the grace of God, of Great Britain, France, and Ireland, King,*
> *Defender of the Faith, etc., Having undertaken, for the Glory*
> *of God and advancement of the Christian Faith and Honour of*
> *our King and Country, a Voyage to plant the First Colony in*
> *the Northern Parts of Virginia; do by these presents solemnly*
> *and mutually in the presence of God and one of another,*
> *Covenant and Combine ourselves together in a Civil Body*
> *Politic . . .*
>
> —MAYFLOWER COMPACT, 1620

THE men who signed the Mayflower Compact, while anchored off Cape Cod in November of 1620, were clear about their duty to the Lord Jesus Christ and to the British king. They were serving both by coming to the New World, and they were determined to establish a government based upon God's laws.

The Pilgrims had come to Cape Cod from the Netherlands, where they had fled years earlier from Britain in order to worship freely outside the authority of the Church of England.

Although they were treated kindly in the Netherlands, they wanted to establish a colony of their own so they could live under God's rule.

They were, however, too poor to emigrate to the New World, and so they appealed for help to the London Company, which owned settlements in Virginia. Sir Edwin Sandys, treasurer of the London Company, agreed to assist them. He solicited investments from his friends to establish a trading company that would finance the Pilgrims' voyage to the New World.

Sandys established the Charter of New England for his new Plymouth Trading Company and was granted authority by the king to establish a trade business in New England. Seventy investors paid for the Pilgrims to travel to New England to establish a trading colony with Britain.[1]

In November 1620, the *Mayflower*, with 102 passengers, dropped anchor off Cape Cod. Before leaving the ship, however, the Pilgrims knew they must establish an agreement about how their colony would operate. In creating the Mayflower Compact, they established self-government for Plymouth Plantation and a society based upon God's laws. The Christian significance of the *Mayflower* is immortalized in a mural in the main Rotunda of our Capitol building. It is one of eight murals, five of which have Christian references. In the *Mayflower* mural is the depiction of a prayer meeting on board the *Mayflower* as it departed from Holland for the New World. An open Bible is at the center of the mural. The murals were placed in the Capitol Rotunda between 1840 and 1855.

Authors Joseph Gaer and Ben Siegel, writing in *The Puritan Heritage: America's Roots in the Bible,* note that the Pilgrims "were motivated primarily by an unassailable determination to worship God according to their own conscience. This determination enabled them to combat the hunger, loneliness, and disease experienced in the New World. Only deep religious conviction can account adequately for the survival of the Plymouth Colony and for the existence of the later Massachusetts Bay, Rhode Island, Maryland, and Pennsylvania colonies."[2]

The Pilgrims made the Bible their political and religious guide and modeled their social organization after Israel's twelve tribes.

Gaer and Siegel note that the Mayflower Compact represented "the first application of a religious covenant to civil government in the New World. No social, religious, or political distinctions were drawn between the Dutch and English groups, or between masters and servants. The government was to promote 'ye generall good of ye Colonie.' "[3]

The compact became the foundational document for our government and was a model for several additional social contracts that led directly to the Declaration of Independence and the Constitution.

The Pilgrim Code of 1656, one of these social contracts, states that the laws given to Israel were "for the mayne so exemplary, being grounded on principles of moral equitie as that all Christians especially ought alwaies to have an eye thereunto in the framing of their politique constitutions."[4]

The Pilgrims were not the only religious group to emigrate to the New World to worship in freedom. In 1629, Puritans from England organized the Massachusetts Bay Company and in April 1630 headed for New England to establish their own colony based upon their understanding of the Bible and how God would have them live.

The Puritans, unlike the Pilgrims, still considered themselves part of the Church of England, but their desire was to reform the church, not leave it.

This Puritan migration to New England was headed by John Winthrop, and 406 carefully screened individuals were chosen to make the trip.

Upon their arrival, they organized their government and social life around the Bible. They, like the Pilgrims, believed they had a covenant with God and that they were to establish a government based upon God's Word.

Despite the Puritans' intolerance toward other religious viewpoints, authors Gaer and Siegel give them credit for establishing the foundation for "our constitutional guarantee of religious freedom in preference to that mere assurance of 'tolerance' that assumes a privileged church. All of us now enjoying the rights and pleasures of American religious, social, and intellectual freedom owe those courageous, tough-minded, passionately devout Puritans—and their Bible—an incalculable debt."[5]

The Puritans were instrumental in forming numerous "friendly societies" that were designed to help care for the community's moral and spiritual well-being. In fact, the Puritan leader Cotton Mather wrote an essay on this subject, "Essay to Do Good," which later inspired Ben Franklin to develop a devotion to public service.

The Pilgrims and Puritans forged Bible-based societies in the New World, but others were to come who would establish colonies based upon religious freedom and freedom of speech.

Religious Belief Flourishes in Other Colonies

Eleven years after the Pilgrims landed in Massachusetts, Roger Williams arrived on the ship *Lyon* in Nantucket along with his wife. Williams began preaching in Boston, Plymouth, and Salem, against the strict rules of the Puritans. He preached that everyone had the right to worship as he pleased and that no one should be forced to attend or support a church against his desires. Williams was one of the first to teach the concept of religious tolerance for others.

Pastor Williams was brought to trial over his preaching. The colonial record of that trial says: "Whereas Mr. Roger Williams, one of the elders of the Church of Salem, hath broached and divulged divers new and dangerous opinions, . . . it is therefore ordered that the said Mr. Williams shall depart . . . within six weeks, . . . not to return anymore without license of the Court."[6]

Roger Williams eventually became a missionary to Indian tribes and established the community of Providence, Rhode Island, as a haven for others who were persecuted for their religious beliefs. In fact, Rhode Island became the home of the first Jewish synagogue in America and a sanctuary for Quakers, who were frequently persecuted in other colonies. Rhode Island also became a refuge for Baptists, who have since become the largest Protestant denomination in the United States.

Religious liberty was also to bloom in Maryland under the guidance of George Calvert, known as Lord Baltimore. He was a close friend of Edwin Sandys, the London Company's treasurer, and both had a commitment to religious freedom.

Calvert, a Catholic, was a secretary of state and adviser to the king when Sandys invited the Pilgrims to settle in New England. Calvert also had a desire to establish a colony that would provide religious freedom to its citizens.

In 1632, King Charles I gave Calvert a grant of land north of the Potomac River. He named it Maryland in honor of the queen, Henrietta Maria. Lord Baltimore was granted full authority to establish whatever kind of government he wished. Baltimore then invited both Catholics and Protestants to settle in his colony and promised them freedom of worship with no taxation to support a state church.

Baltimore also added political liberty to religious liberty. He gave every freeman the right to sit in the government assembly and take part in making the laws of the colony. Religion was not a consideration for holding office in Maryland.

Every governor of Maryland was requested to take an oath that included the promise that he would not question a person's religion. The oath stated that he would find them only, ". . . faithful and well deserving of his said Lordship, and to the best of my understanding, endowed with moral virtues and abilities, fitting for such rewards, offices, or favours, wherein my prime aim and end from time to time, shall sincerely be the advance of his said Lordship's service here . . ."[7]

In guaranteeing religious liberty, Maryland's 1867 declaration of human rights in its constitution says this:

> **Art. 36.** That as it is the duty of every man to worship God in such manner as he thinks most acceptable to Him, all persons are equally entitled to protection in their religious liberty; wherefore, no person ought by any law to be molested in his person or estate, on account of his religious persuasion, or profession, or for his religious practice, unless, under the color of religion, he shall disturb the good order, peace or safety of the State, or shall infringe the laws of morality, or injure others in their natural, civil or religious rights; nor ought any person to be compelled to frequent, or maintain, or contribute, unless on contract, to maintain, any place of worship, or any ministry; nor shall any person, otherwise competent, be deemed incompetent as a witness, or juror, on account of his religious belief; provided, he believes in the existence of God, and that under His dispensation such person will be held morally accountable for his acts, and be rewarded or punished therefore either in this world or in the world to come.[8]

Other Colonies

In Pennsylvania, William Penn, a Quaker, established a colony that was also based upon the Bible—as he understood it—and provided religious liberty to all who vowed to "live peaceably and justly in civil society." In the charter of privileges William Penn granted to Pennsylvania in 1701, he clearly stated the religious nature of Pennsylvania government:

Because no People can be truly happy, though under the greatest Enjoyment of Civil Liberties, if abridged of the Freedom of their Consciences, as to their Religious Profession and Worship; And Almighty God being the only Lord of Conscience, Father of Lights and Spirits; and the Author as well as Object of all divine Knowledge, Faith, and Worship, who only doth enlighten the Minds, and persuade and convince the Understandings of People, I do hereby grant and declare, etc.[9]

One of William Penn's most famous—and true—statements is this: "Those people who are not governed by God will be ruled by tyrants."

Another religiously based colony emerged in what became Connecticut. Under the guidance of Pastor Thomas Hooker in 1638, three towns in Connecticut established their own constitution, known as the "Fundamental Orders."

In the "Fundamental Orders," the authors began with these words: "For as much as it hath pleased Almighty God by the wise disposition of his divine providence so to order and dispose of things that we the Inhabitants and Residents of Windsor, Hartford, and Wethersfield are now cohabiting and dwelling in and upon . . . where a people are gathered together the word of God requires that to maintain the peace and union of such a people there should be an orderly and decent Government established according to God . . ."[10]

The preface to the "Fundamental Orders" also says that the people of these towns were joined together "to maintain and preserve the liberty and purity of the Gospel of our Lord Jesus," and that their "civil affairs" were to be guided by the laws decreed in the constitution they were signing.

A few months prior to the enactment of the Connecticut Fundamental Orders, the general assembly invited Pastor Hooker to speak to them. There is no historical text of his sermon left, but one eyewitness outlined the main points of Hooker's speech. The eyewitness was 28-year-old Henry Wolcott, whose partial outline is reprinted here:

1. The choice of public magistrates belongs unto the people by God's own allowance.
2. The election must be conducted by the people, but votes should not be cast "in accord with their humors, but according to the will and law of God."
3. Those who "have the power to appoint officers and magistrates also have the power to set bounds and limitations on their power" so that "the foundation of authority is laid in the free consent of the people," because "by a free choice the hearts of the people will be more inclined to the love of the persons chosen, and more ready to yield obedience.[11]

Historian Benjamin Hart, writing in *The Christian Roots of American Liberty*, devotes an entire chapter to Pastor Hooker because of the pivotal role he played in American history. According to Hart, Hooker's writings inspired Thomas Jefferson in laying the foundations for our republican form of government.

Yet, says Hart, Hooker's primary desire in establishing Connecticut was not politically motivated. It was his desire to create a more perfect Christian culture than he had yet seen in the New World.

Hart says there was a consistent pattern in the formation of new colonies throughout New England, ". . . with each colony attempting to create a more pristine Christian society, and each founder, usually a minister, trying to 'out-Protestantize' everyone else."[12]

Pastor Hooker's contribution to the "Fundamental Orders" and to the formation of our republican form of government—with religious freedom guaranteed for all—cannot be underestimated. According to Benjamin Hart, "The Fundamental Orders of Connecticut was the most advanced government charter the world had ever seen in terms of guaranteeing individual rights," however, ". . . its primary purpose in the minds of the people of Connecticut was to establish a commonwealth according to God's laws and to create an environment conducive to spreading the Gospel."[13]

The First Charter of Virginia, which was granted by King James I in 1606, stated the following:

> We, greatly commending, and graciously accepting of, their Desires for the Furtherance of so noble a Work, which may, by the Providence of Almighty God, hereafter tend to the Glory of his Divine Majesty, in propagating of Christian Religion to such People, as yet live in Darkness and miserable Ignorance of the true Knowledge and Worship of God, and may in time bring the Infidels and Savages, living in those parts, to human Civility, and to a settled and quiet Government; Do, by these our Letters Patents, graciously accept of, and agree to, their humble and well-intended Desires.[14]

In 1776, Virginia passed the Virginia Bill of Rights, authored by George Mason. Four years before the Declaration of Independence was published, Mason argued before the General Court of Virginia: "All acts of legislature apparently contrary to natural right and justice are, in our laws, and must be in the nature of things, considered as void. The laws of nature are the laws of God, whose authority can be superseded by no power on earth. A legislature must not obstruct our obedience to Him from whose punishments they cannot protect us. All human constitutions which contradict His laws, we are in conscience bound to disobey."[15] Mason understood the relationship between religion and political freedom.

In 1786 in Virginia, Thomas Jefferson crafted the Virginia Act for Establishing Religious Freedom, which influenced the thinking of the Founders in the writing of the Constitution and Bill of Rights. Christianity was considered the main religious belief in the New World and the protection of religious belief became a high priority among the colonists—regardless of their particular denominational background.[16]

Jefferson's document outlines the reasons why religious freedom must be protected and he states why "truth is great and will prevail if left to herself" in debates over religious viewpoints.

The document states that, ". . . no man shall be compelled to frequent or support any religious worship, place, or ministry whatsoever, nor shall be enforced, restrained, molested, or burdened in his body or goods, nor shall otherwise suffer on account of his religious opinions or belief; but that all men shall be free to profess, and by argument to maintain, their opinions in matters of religion, and that the same shall in nowise diminish, enlarge, or affect their civil capacities."

The Declaration of Independence and the Constitution

As the colonies debated declaring their independence from England, the American revolutionaries chose Thomas Jefferson to write a declaration of independence from the king of England. The colonies knew such a declaration meant war.

With this in mind, Jefferson wrote these words:

We hold these truths to be self-evident that all men are created equal, that they are endowed by their Creator with certain unalienable Rights, that among these are life, liberty and the pursuit of Happiness. That to serve these rights, Governments are instituted among Men, deriving their just powers from the consent of the governed. That whenever any Form of Government becomes destructive of these ends, it is the right of the people to alter or abolish it.[17]

The Declaration was very clear in its assertion that God has given men certain unalienable rights and that governments are simply to be instruments to serve God in creating an orderly and just society.

The Declaration declared that when leaders begin usurping or violating the rights of the governed, it is the right of the people to alter or abolish that tyrannical government. It also stated it was the right of individuals to form governments and to elect their leaders. These were revolutionary statements that King George did not accept well.

Following the War of Independence victory, the new Continental Congress of the United States drafted the Articles of Confederation that lacked both a federal system and guarantees of personal liberties. Unable to act as one nation and with the laws of states in contradiction, a Constitutional Convention later created our current Constitution, including the first ten amendments—commonly referred to as the Bill of Rights.

The First Amendment in the Bill of Rights guaranteed religious freedom, freedom of speech, and freedom of the press—essential rights in a self-governing nation. The First Amendment's statement on religious freedom, which has been twisted and distorted by secularists for decades, was designed to prohibit the establishment of a national church—not to build an impenetrable "wall of separation" between church and state. The amendment was designed to protect religious freedom, not restrict it. It says:

Congress shall make no law respecting an establishment of religion, or prohibiting the free exercise thereof; or abridging the freedom of speech, or of the press; or the right of the people peaceably to assemble, and to petition the Government for a redress of grievances.[18]

The Founding Fathers clearly understood the importance of religious and political freedom. In fact, many of them openly expressed the view that our republican form of government was only designed for a Christian or moral people—not for any others. Their view was that self-government could only survive if individuals were guided by a belief in God. A federal government of limited powers could function properly when people were self-governed and believed that they owed their lives and futures to God. A self-governing people do not need a web of external laws to force them to be good or to behave in a civil manner. Their religious beliefs will accomplish what laws can never accomplish.

The influence of Christians upon the founding of our nation and the writing of our basic documents cannot be overestimated. Dr. James Hutson, author of *Religion and the Founding of the American Republic*, observed that it was John Dickinson, a member of Congress in 1776, who wrote the first draft of the Articles of Confederation. Dickinson later retired from public life to devote himself to writing commentaries on the gospel of Matthew and other religious endeavors.[19]

In addition, Elias Boudinot, the president of Congress from 1782–1783, wrote religious tracts and became the first president of the American Bible Society in 1816.

John Jay, who served as president of Congress and a justice of the Supreme Court, eventually headed the American Bible Society also.

At the first meeting of the Congress in September 1774, one of its first orders of business was to find a minister to open its sessions with prayer. They picked Anglican Reverend Jacob Duche, who served through 1776. In addition, on June 12, 1775, Congress had issued a resolution calling for a day of "public humiliation, fasting and prayer."

Congress was also concerned about the interrupted supply of Bibles from England during the War of Independence. Acting on the encouragement of three Presbyterian ministers, Congress approved the purchase of 20,000 Bibles to be imported from Europe—but the order was never carried out because the British were on the verge of capturing Philadelphia.

Dr. Hutson also points out a little known fact of history: Church services in the House of Representatives "began as soon as the government moved to Washington, in the fall of 1800." In fact, "Services in the Capitol continued . . . into the 1850s, long after Washington teemed with churches. From 1865–1868 (just after the Civil War), the House permitted the newly organized First Congregational Church of Washington to use its chambers for church and Sunday School services, at precisely the time, May 13, 1866, when Congress passed the Fourteenth Amendment, which, according to some later judicial theories, forbids religious activities on public property."[20]

What's the Relationship between God and Government?

As noted earlier, the founders knew that good government could only exist as long as the citizens were moral and believed in an almighty God.

Charles Carroll, a signer of the Declaration of Independence, for example, said this: "Without morals a Republic cannot subsist any length of time; they therefore who are decrying the Christian religion . . . are undermining the solid morals, the best security for the duration of free government."[21]

Gouverneur Morris, a signer of the Constitution, said: "There must be religion. When that ligament is torn, society is disjointed and its members perish. The nation is exposed to foreign violence and domestic convulsion."[22]

Benjamin Rush, a signer of the Declaration of Independence, said: "I have been alternately called an aristocrat and a democrat. I am now neither. I am a Christocrat . . . He alone who created and redeemed man is qualified to govern him."[23]

President John Adams said of the Constitution: "Our Constitution was made only for a moral and religious people. It is wholly inadequate to the government of any other."[24]

James Madison, who would become our fourth president, wrote in 1785, "We have staked the future of all our political institutions upon the capacity of mankind for self-government; upon the capacity of each and all of us to govern ourselves, to control ourselves, to sustain ourselves, according to the Ten Commandments of God."[25]

William Linn, the chaplain of the House of Representatives in 1789, warned of the dangers of trying to govern without God: "Let my neighbor once persuade himself that there is no God, and he will soon pick my pocket, and break not only my leg but my neck. If there be no God, there is no law, no future account; government then is ordinance of man only, and we cannot be subject to conscience' sake."[26]

These men clearly understood what most Americans no longer do: that Christianity and an adherence to God's laws are the building blocks upon which civilized nations function. America was founded directly upon a covenant with God and a belief that the Bible provided the early settlers with a clear guidebook to use in forming a just and lasting civilization for the propagation of the Gospel.

That we have lost this consciousness of our history does not make it less true. It is essential that we renew our commitment to seeing that we function as a nation under God—and that we do whatever is legally necessary to make certain "under God" remains in the Pledge of Allegiance; that we restore prayer in schools; and that we make certain that no militant atheist succeeds in removing "In God We Trust" from our coins and paper currency.

We Were a Christian Nation

In 1892, the same year the Pledge of Allegiance was first published, the U.S. Supreme Court issued a ruling stating that America has always been a religious nation.

The case is *Holy Trinity Church v. United States* and involved the desire of that New York church to hire a minister from a foreign country. The hiring of the minister conflicted with a law passed by Congress forbidding U.S. citizens from contracting labor from foreigners.

Supreme Court Justice David Brewer wrote the majority opinion for the Court in *Holy Trinity*. In the Court's opinion, Brewer had surveyed the founding documents of our nation, including state constitutions, and public pronouncements of the Founding Fathers on the relationship between Christianity and the establishment of the United States.

Justice Brewer made the following declarations in his opinion:

> . . . this is a religious people. This is historically true. From the discovery of this continent to the present hour, there is a single voice making this affirmation. The commission to Christopher Columbus, prior to his sail westward, is from "Ferdinand and Isabella, by the grace of God, king and queen of Castile," etc., and recites that "it is hoped that by God's assistance some of the continents and islands in the ocean will be discovered," etc. The first colonial grant, that made to Sir Walter Raleigh in 1584, was from "Elizabeth, by the grace of God, of England, France and Ireland, queen, defender of the faith," etc.; and the grant authorizing him to enact statutes of the government of the proposed colony provided that "they be not against the true Christian faith now professed in the Church of England."

Even the constitution of the United States, which is supposed to have little touch upon the private life of the individual, contains in the first amendment a declaration common to the constitutions of all the states, as follows: "Congress shall make no law respecting an establishment of religion, or prohibiting the free exercise thereof," etc.— and also provides in article 1, 7, (a provision common to many constitutions,) that the executive shall have 10 days (Sundays excepted) within which to determine whether he will approve or veto a bill.

* * *

There is no dissonance in these declarations. There is a universal language pervading them all, having one meaning. They affirm and reaffirm that this is a religious nation. These are not individual sayings, declarations of private persons. They are organic utterances. They speak the voice of the entire people. While because of a general recognition of this truth the question has seldom been presented to the courts, yet we find that in Updegraph v. Com., 11 Serg. & R. 394, 400, it was decided that, "Christianity, general Christianity, is, and always has been, a part of the common law of Pennsylvania; . . . not Christianity with an established church and tithes and spiritual courts, but Christianity with liberty of conscience to all men." And in People v. Ruggles, 8 Johns. 290, 294, 295, Chancellor KENT, the great commentator on American law, speaking as chief justice of the supreme court of New York, said: "The people of this state, in common with the people of this country, profess the general doctrines of Christianity as the rule of their faith and practice; and to scandalize the author of these doctrines is not only, in a religious point of view, extremely impious, but, even in respect to the obligations due to society, is a gross violation of decency and good order. . . . The free, equal, and undisturbed enjoyment of religious opinion, whatever it may be, and free and decent discussions on any religious subject, is granted and secured; but to revile, with malicious and blasphemous contempt, the religion professed by almost the whole community is an abuse of that right. Nor are we bound by any expressions in the constitution, as some have strangely supposed, either not to punish at all, or to punish indiscriminately the like attacks upon the religion of Mahomet or of the Grand Lama; and for this plain reason, that the case assumes that we are a Christian people, and the morality of the country is deeply ingrafted upon Christianity, and not upon the doctrines or worship of those impostors." And in the famous case of Vidal v. Girard's Ex'rs, 2 How. 127, 198, this court, while sustaining the will of Mr. Girard, with its provision for the creation of a college into which no minister should be permitted to enter, observed: "It is also said, and truly, that the Christian religion is a part of the common law of Pennsylvania."

If we pass beyond these matters to a view of American life, as expressed by its laws, its business, its customs, and its society, we find everywhere a clear recognition of the same truth. Among other matters note the following: The form of oath universally prevailing, concluding with an appeal to the Almighty; the custom of opening sessions of all deliberative bodies and most conventions with prayer; the prefatory words of all wills, "In the name of God, amen;" the laws respecting the observance of the Sabbath, with the general cessation of all secular business, and the closing of courts, legislatures, and other similar public assemblies on that day; the churches and church organizations which abound in every city, town, and hamlet; the multitude of charitable organizations existing every where under Christian auspices; the gigantic missionary associations, with general support, and aiming to establish Christian missions in every quarter of the globe. These, and many other matters which might be noticed, add a volume of unofficial declarations to the mass of organic utterances that this is a Christian nation. In the face of all these, shall it be believed that a congress of the United States intended to make it a misdemeanor for a church of this country to contract for the services of a Christian minister residing in another nation?[27]

Justice Brewer elaborated on this opinion in a small volume titled *The United States: A Christian Nation,* published in 1905. In it, Brewer stated that his proposition wasn't that Christianity was the state religion, but that Christianity "was the primary cause of the first settlement on our shores; that the organic instruments, charters, and constitutions of the colonies were filled with abundant recognitions of it as a controlling factor in the life of the people."[28]

Brewer noted as well that even though our nation was founded upon Christian principles, ". . . all religions have free scope within our borders. Numbers of our people profess other religions, and many reject all."[29] In short, America's Christian foundations provided freedom of worship for all religions—not just Christianity.

Justice Brewer's view of American history was also affirmed decades earlier by historian B. F. Morris in his book *The Christian Life and Character of the Civil Institutions of the United States,* published in 1863. Morris wrote the following:

The Christian faith and character of the men who formed the Constitution forbid the idea that they designed not only to place the Constitution and its government under the providence and protection of God and the principles of the Christian religion. In all their previous state papers they had declared Christianity to be fundamental to the well-being of society and government, and in every form of official authority had stated this fact. . . . The various states who had sent these good and great men to the convention to form a Constitution had, in all their civil charters, expressed, as states and as a people, their faith in God and the Christian religion. Most of the statesmen themselves were Christian men; and the convention had for its president George Washington, who had everywhere paid a public homage to the Christian religion.[30]

As we have seen from this brief overview of the history of various colonies in the New World, the leaders of these colonies were Christians who believed they were establishing civil societies under God's laws. While several of the early colonies were restrictive in their commitment to particular religious beliefs, the ones formed later were specifically created to permit freedom of religion as the basis of good government and a peaceful civil society. Freedom to worship as one pleased, without coercion, became a hallmark of these colonies and they flourished under this basic concept.

These concepts were eventually incorporated into our fundamental documents in forming the United States of America. This nation was founded "under God" from the very beginning. Our Declaration of Independence, Constitution, laws, and state constitutions were founded on the premise that God rules over men and that we must have an orderly government based upon God's moral laws.

CHAPTER 2

God and Concepts
Of Government

We have no government armed with power capable of contending with human passions unbridled by morality and religion. Avarice, ambition, revenge, or gallantry, would break the strongest cords of our Constitution as a whale goes through a net. Our Constitution was made only for a moral and religious people. It is wholly inadequate to the government of any other.

—PRESIDENT JOHN ADAMS, October 11, 1798

JOHN Adams knew the importance of religion being the moral glue that would hold the republic together. In a letter to Thomas Jefferson, Adams wrote: "Have you ever found in history, one single example of a Nation thoroughly corrupted that was afterwards restored to virtue? . . . And without virtue, there can be no political liberty."[1]

Adams, along with many of the other founders, along with the Pilgrims and the Puritans before them, knew that the citizens of the colonies and later the republic could only survive in freedom if they were a virtuous people who believed in Jesus Christ as their Lord. (Some of the Founding Fathers were deists and not necessarily believers in Jesus Christ.)

They understood, as most Americans do not, that freedom can only survive when individuals are self-governing and responsible for their own behaviors. To the founders, political freedom was forever linked to religious belief and practice. One could not exist without the other.

Our nation was founded upon the Bible and the four basic forms of government outlined in the Bible (excluding self-government). The Puritans, Pilgrims, and the Founding Fathers understood these forms of government to be: God's law, civil government, the family, and the church. All these governments were to be based upon God's laws, and the early settlers in the New World organized their lives around these four distinct—but interrelated—governments.

God's Law

The Pilgrims and the Puritans had a clear vision of their calling from God to establish a civil government under the rule of God's laws. They believed that the Old Testament contained explicit instructions on how God wished civil governments to operate.

Hebraic culture, as established under Moses and the judges, was the model the Puritans and Pilgrims used in forming their civil governments. The Ten Commandments were taken seriously by the Israelites and covered such matters as adultery, murder, worshipping false idols, not respecting parents, stealing, false accusations, greed, and using God's name in vain.

Under the Hebraic system, God's law was the final authority on all matters. The Israelites had the Ten Commandments as well as the various Levitical laws they and the priests were required to obey. The rules in Leviticus covered all manner of issues involving morality and the worship of God. They included such commands as those in Leviticus 19:11–13: "Do not steal or cheat or lie. Do not make a promise in my name if you do not intend to keep it; that brings disgrace on my name. I am the Lord your God. Do not take advantage of anyone or rob him. Do not hold back the wages of someone you have hired, not even for one night." Exodus 21 and 22 contain numerous verses that outline God's views on such issues as premeditated murder, manslaughter, assault, abortion, infanticide, property crimes, criminal negligence, parenting, robbery, and other issues. Chapters 17 through 22 of Deuteronomy deal with violating court orders, malicious accusations, building codes, juvenile delinquency, rape, and more.

God gave the Israelites explicit instructions on how to order their society, maintain justice, protect the innocent, punish the guilty, and live peaceably with others. These instructions were adopted by the Puritans and Pilgrims as a way of creating an orderly and just society in the New World.

In *The Puritan Heritage: America's Roots in the Bible*, historians Joseph Gaer and Ben Siegel note that the Puritan government official "viewed both natural and biblical law as God's primary means of imposing upon fallen man the divine will."[2]

As time passed, Christian philosophers, lawyers, and statesmen developed a thoroughly biblical worldview of how God's law was to apply to the lives of those in the colonies—and later to the republic. In particular, four men had tremendous influence on the thinking of our founders: Samuel Rutherford, John Locke, William Blackstone, and Algernon Sidney. Each of these men understood that the New World was "under God" and had a divine mission to enable men to live in freedom in a self-governing system.

Civil Government

William Blackstone's *Commentaries on the Laws of England* had a profound impact on the thinking of the Founding Fathers. Dr. Robert Stacey, a professor of government at Patrick Henry College, authored *Sir William Blackstone and the Common Law*. Stacey says Blackstone's *Commentaries* helped develop the legal theory that properly balances the rights of the individual with the rights of the community. Blackstone, says Stacey, "was a serious and devout Christian who saw God's law as the foundation of all just human law, and so the Bible was central" to all law.

Blackstone wrote that the law of nature (God's law) was "superior to any other. It is binding over all the globe in all countries, and at all times; no human laws are of any validity, if contrary to this; and such of them as are valid derive all their force, and all their authority, mediately or immediately, from this original."[3]

The Blackstone Institute, a Christian-based group dedicated to the preservation of Blackstone's legacy, has outlined some of the key theological and legal thoughts in his writings. Blackstone taught that there are six basic types of law—and all are God-ordained: law as order of the universe, law as a rule of human action, law of nature, revealed law, laws of nations, and municipal laws.

In addition, Blackstone wrote that God has built into the universe immutable laws that must be obeyed. God created these laws for the benefit of mankind and only when people obey these laws will they be happy. Human laws must be based upon God's revealed laws in order for mankind to live in peace and harmony.

Another strong voice was Algernon Sidney. His ideas inclined the view of the Founding Fathers toward a republican, or representative, form of government. Sidney was born in 1622 and elected to the British parliament in 1646. He wrote a classic work entitled *Discourses Concerning Government*, which was published in 1698, fifteen years after his death.

Sidney wrote *Discourses* between 1680 and 1683 in response to a book by Robert Filmer called *Patriarcha*, which supported the divine right of kings.

Sidney's *Discourses* argued for the rights of men to govern themselves and to establish representative forms of government. He also upheld the right of citizens to revolt against tyrannical regimes. One of his more famous quotes is this: "We are free-men governed by our own laws, and . . . no man has a power over us, which is not given and regulated by them."[4]

Sidney has been called the "Forgotten Founding Father" because of his powerful influence on the thinking of John Adams, Samuel Adams, George Mason, James Madison, Benjamin Franklin, and other founders of our nation.

Sidney's idea that government is a contract between the leaders and the people was adopted by the Founding Fathers. In *Discourses* he wrote, "God leaves to Man the choice of Forms in Government; and those who constitute one Form, may abrogate it. . . . The general revolt of a Nation cannot be called a Rebellion. . . . Laws and constitutions ought to be weighed . . . to constitute that which is most conducing to the establishment of justice and liberty."[5] In 1677 Sidney began working with William Penn to promote religious liberty both in America and in England.

Sidney's reputation as a philosopher who influenced the American Revolution was so obvious during that time that a group of Virginians, including Patrick Henry, founded Hampden-Sydney College in 1776 in his honor and that of John Hampden who was mortally wounded in the battle of Chalgrove Field fighting for the cause of parliamentary government against a despotic king in 1643. In 1825, Thomas Jefferson, as founder of the University of Virginia, said that Sidney's thoughts in his *Discourses* "may be considered as those generally approved by our fellow citizens of this state, and the United States." The state of Massachusetts adopted one of his sayings as the state motto: "By the sword we seek peace, but peace only under liberty." The American abolitionist William Lloyd Garrison was inspired by a quote from Sidney: "That which is not just, is not Law; and that which is not Law, ought not to be obeyed."[6]

Regrettably, Sidney was beheaded in 1683 for allegedly attempting to help a group of rebels assassinate King Charles II.

If he had lived, it is likely he would have written far more about his belief that governments derive their power from the consent of the governed.

Another person with significant influence upon the thinking of the Founding Fathers was the English philosopher John Locke, who was born in 1632. Locke's two most famous essays, *Two Treatises of Government* and *Treatise on Government,* both inspired the Founders in their efforts to free the New World from the tyranny of English rule. So closely did the Founding Fathers read Locke's works that Henry Lee, one of the signers of the Declaration of Independence, said that the Declaration itself was "copied from Locke's *Treatise on Government.*" Comparing the following words of Locke with those of Jefferson in the Declaration, it is easy to see Lee's point:

> Secondly: I answer, such revolutions happen not upon every little mismanagement in public affairs. Great mistakes in the ruling part, many wrong and inconvenient laws, and all the slips of human frailty will be borne by the people without mutiny or murmur. But if a long train of abuses, prevarications, and artifices, all tending the same way, make the design visible to the people, and they cannot but feel what they lie under, and see whither they are going, it is not to be wondered that they should then rouse themselves, and endeavor to put the rule into such hands which may secure to them the end for which government was at first erected. . . .[7]

Jefferson's words in the Declaration states:

> Prudence, indeed, will dictate that Governments long established should not be changed for light and transient causes; and accordingly all experience hath shown, that mankind are more disposed to suffer, while evils are suf-

ferable, than to right themselves by abolishing the forms to which they are accustomed. But when a long train of abuses and usurpations, pursuing invariably the same Object evinces a design to reduce them under absolute Despotism, it is their right, it is their duty, to throw off such Government, and to provide new Guards for their future security.[8]

John Locke argued in his works that governments can only be built upon the unchanging principles of natural law, which are a subset of God's laws. He declared: "The Law of Nature stands as an eternal rule to all men, legislators as well as others. The rules that they make for other men's actions must . . . be conformable to the Law of Nature, i.e., to the will of God."[9]

The early twentieth-century historian C. Edward Merriam, writing in *A History of American Political Theories*, said this of John Locke's influence on the Founders:

> Locke, in particular, was the authority to whom the Patriots paid greatest deference. He was the most famous of seventeenth century democratic theorists, and his ideas had their due weight with the colonists. Almost every writer seems to have been influenced by him, many quoted his words, and the argument of others shows the unmistakable imprint of his philosophy. . . . No one stated more strongly than did he the basis for the doctrine that "taxation without representation is tyranny." No better epitome of the Revolutionary theory could be found than in John Locke on civil government.[10]

Locke not only wrote about civil government, but about his Christian beliefs. He wrote a commentary on Paul's epistles; created a topical Bible; and wrote an important essay titled "The Reasonableness of Christianity as Delivered in the Scriptures."

(Many of Locke's political ideas were drawn from the work of the British theologian Richard Hooker [1554–1600].)

In Locke's two treatises on civil government, he quotes from the Bible 1,506 times—1,349 times in his first essay and 157 times in the second. Locke once wrote of the Bible: "The holy Scripture is to me and always will be the constant guide of assent; and I shall always hearken to it as containing infallible truth relating to things of highest concernment . . . and I shall immediately condemn and quit any opinion of mine, as soon as I am shown that it is contrary to any revelation in the holy scripture."[11]

Another who significantly influenced the minds of our founders was Samuel Rutherford, author of *Lex Rex* in 1644. *Lex Rex* means "the law is king." John Locke had drawn heavily on Rutherford's revolutionary work. Rutherford's book asserted that no one—not even the king—is above the law. And law, of course, had to be based upon God's Word in order to be valid over individuals and nations.

The late Dr. Francis Schaeffer in his classic work *The Christian Manifesto* (1982) describes the revolutionary ideas proposed by Rutherford in *Lex Rex* and the amazing impact his thoughts had on the American Revolution. Schaeffer summarized Rutherford's basic premise:

> What is the concept in *Lex Rex*? Very simply: The law is king, and if the king and the government disobey the law they are to be disobeyed. And the law is founded on the Law of God. *Lex Rex* was outlawed in both England and Scotland. The parliament of Scotland met together in 1661 in order to condemn Samuel Rutherford to death for treason, and the only reason he was not executed as a civil rebel is because he died first.[12]

Rutherford argued that Romans 13 says all power is from God and that government is ordained and instituted by

God. Acts of the government that contradict God's laws should be disobeyed. A government without God's sanction is a tyranny.

According to Rutherford, ". . . a power ethical, politic, or moral, to oppress, is not from God, and is not a power, but a licentious deviation of a power; and is no more from God, but from sinful nature and the old serpent, than a license to sin." Rutherford also argued that to resist governments without God is to honor God! *Lex Rex* asserted that civil magistrates hold their authority as representatives of the people and that if the governmental leaders violate this trust, they must be resisted.

Rutherford laid out a way for citizens to resist tyranny. First, they can defend themselves through protests; second, they can flee from persecution if necessary; and third, they can use force to defend themselves from tyrannical government.

Rutherford and later Locke made several points about the relationship between citizens and their government:

1. We have inalienable rights from God.
2. The government is established by the consent of the governed.
3. There is a separation of powers in government in order to decentralize power.
4. There is a right to revolution if the government becomes a tyranny.[13]

These ideas became the "fire in the minds" of the Founding Fathers when they issued the declaration of our independence from English rule and later crafted the Constitution to protect individual liberties and establish a representative government! They built our republican form of government upon the belief that individuals and nations are "under God" and that only a religious people can sustain a free society.

The Family

In the twenty-first century, it is probably an oddity to talk of the family as a government, but the Bible clearly considers it the foundational government of a society for the nurturing of children to become lovers of God and good citizens. When God created Adam and Eve and placed them in the Garden of Eden, he established the first family as well as the first government.

In Genesis 1:26–28 and 2:20–25, God ordained that Adam and Eve should have many children who would spread throughout the earth controlling the environment and animals. The Old Testament describes the patriarchal society of the Israelites and the importance of tribes that eventually grew into cities and then nation-states.

The biblical model of the family was adopted by the Puritans and Pilgrims, and this model was accepted as normal in Colonial America. The Pilgrims and Puritans understood what most twenty-first century Americans do not: Strong families are the basic units of a society and godly families impact the culture and the government.

In 1693, one Massachusetts cleric stated: "The Foundation of a whole People's or Kingdom's reformation or defection, religion or rebellion is laid in families. Families are the constituent parts of nations and kingdoms; hence as families are well or ill disciplined, so will be the whole be well disposed or ill inclined."[14] Puritan leader Cotton Mather knew the relationship between the government of the family and the civil government. In 1707, he asked: "In a family where good orders are kept and prayer is every morning and evening seriously carried on, are not the children and servants likely to be more orderly, more dutiful, more virtuous, than in a family where God is not sought unto? And are not religious families likely to be the best support and safety for the Common-wealth?"[15] The answer, of course, was obvious to Mather and other Puritan leaders.

Education Was to Play a Role

The Puritans understood the importance of the family in training godly children to become godly citizens. They also knew that schools and colleges could play a role in training children to serve the Lord and to become well-informed self-governed citizens.

In 1636, the Puritans founded Harvard College as an institution not only to train the younger generation in the ways of the Lord, but to develop an educated clergy for the spreading of the gospel throughout the New World. Harvard students received a thorough training in Hebrew and Greek so they could rightly interpret the Bible. Later, Yale was founded with the purpose of training ministers and an educated citizenry. Yale's original seal depicted an open Bible with the Hebrew inscription "Light and Truth" over it. King's College (now Columbia University) was founded for the purpose of teaching "the principles of Christianity and Morality generally agreed upon."[16]

In 1642, the Massachusetts legislature passed a law requiring parents to be responsible for the elementary school education of their children. The law said that parents must teach their children and indentured servants "to read the english tongue, and knowledge of the Capital laws: upon penaltie of twentie shillings for each neglect therein. Also that all masters of families do once a week (at the Least) catechize their children and servants in the grounds and principles of Religion."[17]

And in 1647, the Massachusetts legislature passed a bill making education a public responsibility. In the preamble to this act, it stated that education was the means of enhancing spiritual health: "It being one chief project of that old deluder, Satan, to keep men from the knowledge of Scriptures, as in former times keeping them in an unknown tongue."[18]

The primary purpose of parental and institutional education in early America was to teach children to love and serve God and to become good citizens. This concept lived on through the Revolutionary War. In fact, Dr. Benjamin Rush, one of the signers of the Declaration of Independence, urged the use of the Bible in all public schools. In his essay "A Defense of the Use of the Bible as a School Book," Rush said the Bible would teach children democratic principles and a code of proper moral values to follow in life.

In 1690, to aid in the training of children with a Christian worldview, Benjamin Harris published *The New England Primer,* a textbook that was used in both public and private schools in America from 1690 through 1900. The textbook reads like a Bible catechism, with various essays and articles on Christian morality and faith. The 1777 version, which has been reprinted on the Internet, teaches children the alphabet by a series of rhymes beginning with "A: In Adam's Fall We sinned All" and ending with Z: Zaccheus he Did climb the Tree Our Lord to See."[19]

The 1777 version also includes an "Alphabet of Lessons for Youth" featuring quotations from the Old and New Testaments, including "Except a man be born again, he cannot see the kingdom of God." It also includes a catechism for children that begins with the question: "What is the chief end of man? Answer: Man's chief end is to glorify God and enjoy him forever."[20]

In the colonies, the prevailing belief among America's political, educational, and ministry leaders was that Christianity was to be taught in the homes, in the schools, and in the churches as a guarantee that the nation would train future generations to love the Lord, be self-governed by the laws of God, and understand and participate in our republican form of government. This view of education is a far cry from today's claim by secular humanists that the Constitution requires a complete separation of church and state! The fact is that the writers of the Constitution and the First Amendment opposed a national state church, but had no problem whatsoever with Christian religious principles being infused into governmental policies and the education of America's youth.

The fact that the *New England Primer* was so widely and consistently used in schools throughout America up until the twentieth century clearly shows that there were no "constitutional" issues involving separation of church and state in the minds of Americans.

Shortly after the Revolution Bibles were in short supply and Congress passed a resolution in 1781 to commend their printing in the United States which read: "Resolved, That the United States in Congress assembled, highly approve the pious and laudable undertaking of Mr. Aitken as subservient to the interest of religion as well as the progress of the arts in this country, and being satisfied from the above report, of his care and accuracy, in the execution of the work, they recommend this edition of the Bible to the inhabitants of the United States, and hereby authorize him to publish this recommendation in the manner he shall think proper."

President Jefferson signed a treaty with the Kaskaskia Indians that was ratified by Congress that paid an annual subsidy for a priest because most of the Indians had become Christians (http://digital.library.okstate.edu/KAPPLER/Vol2/treaties/kas0067.htm).

This situation changed in 1947, because of a badly flawed and wrongly decided Supreme Court decision, which will be discussed in detail in Chapter 6. Because of this 1947 decision, *Everson v. Board of Education*—and subsequent decisions—our nation is faced with all of the controversies over the alleged "separation of church and state" and the new battle over whether the Pledge of Allegiance is "unconstitutional" because it contains the words "under God."

The Church

The Pilgrims and Puritans had no problem in linking the institution of the church with the state. To their thinking, it was their God-ordained duty to establish colonies in the New World that had civil governments based upon the Word of God.

Puritan leader John Winthrop made this clear in a sermon he preached to his fellow Puritans on the ship *Arabella*, shortly after it left England for the New World. He told them they were chosen by God and that ". . . we must consider that we shall be as a City upon a Hill, the eyes of all people are upon us."

In 1645, Winthrop gave a speech setting out the religious philosophy of his colony. He told his Puritan followers they had liberty only to do that which was good, just, and honest. "This liberty," said Winthrop, "is maintained and exercised in a way of subjection to authority, it is the same kind of liberty whereof Christ hath made us free. . . . If you stand for your natural corrupt liberties, and will do what is good in your own eyes, you will not endure the least weight of authority . . . but if you will be satisfied to enjoy such civil and lawful liberties, such as Christ allows you, then you will quietly and cheerfully submit unto that authority which is set over you . . . for your good."[21]

Religion, then, was not only a private matter, but a public matter as well. William Penn agreed with this. In 1682, he wrote: "Government seems to me a part of religion itself, a thing sacred in its institution and end. . . . It crushes the effects of evil and is as such (though lower yet) an emanation of the same divine power that is both author and object of pure religion, government itself being otherwise as capable of kindness, goodness, and charity as a more private society."[22] In the early settlements in the New World, the civil governments had authority to punish religious offenses as well as secular ones.

But what role did the church and ministers play in the New World and in civil governments? Ministers understood that their role was to teach God's people, and to enforce accountability within the church. They knew they were given authority by God to preach the gospel as well as good citizenship. However, they also understood that the civil government had a separate authority and function that included punishing evildoers, defending the community, and keeping local governments functioning properly.

According to historians Joseph Gaer and Ben Siegel in *The Puritan Heritage: America's Roots in the Bible*, "A definite distinction between the church and commonwealth officers developed when shortly after their arrival in New England the ministers surrendered judicial office. They had decided that for them to serve as magistrates was to contradict God's word. However, they had no intention of abandoning their unofficial authority and influence. They not only discussed community policy among themselves, but they consulted frequently with the magistrates, to whom they assigned the choicest seats in church and to whom they regularly offered advice."[23]

The ministers of the gospel took a leading role in preparing the American people for the revolution against England. In fact, the British dubbed them the "Black Regiment" for their black robes and their key role in fomenting the war of independence from British tyranny.

The pulpits of America rang forth with sermon after sermon about the biblical justification for resistance to tyranny as being service to God! The ministers laid the philosophical groundwork for their congregations to rally behind the Founding Fathers in their efforts to throw off British rule.

Historian Dr. James Hutson, writing in *Religion and the Founding of the American Republic*, has observed of the Revolutionary War–era pastors:

> Preachers seemed to vie with their brethren in other colonies in arousing their congregations against George III. In 1775, John Adams informed friends in New England that the ministers of Philadelphia "thunder and lighten every Sabbath" against British tyranny, while Jefferson reported that in Virginia "pulpit oratory ran 'like a shock of electricity' through the whole colony." In this atmosphere, it is not surprising that a British agent in New York in March 1776 concluded that "at bottom [this] was very

much a religious War," an observation supported recently by a British historian who has called the American Revolution "the last great war of religion in the western world."[24]

To give the reader a flavor of the kinds of sermons being preached by pastors before and at the beginning of the Revolutionary War, I am reprinting a portion of a sermon given by Samuel Langdon before the Congress of the Colony of Massachusetts on May 31, 1775, just a few weeks after the American War of Independence began on Lexington Green (April 19):

We have used our utmost endeavors, by repeated humble petitions and remonstrances, by a series of unanswerable reasonings published from the press—in which the dispute has been fairly stated, and the justice of our opposition clearly demonstrated,—and by the mediation of some of the nobles and most faithful friends of the British constitution, who have powerfully pleaded our cause in Parliament, to prevent such measures as may soon reduce the body politic to a miserable, dismembered, dying trunk, though lately the terror of all Europe. But our king, as if impelled by some strange fatality, is resolved to reason with us only by the roar of his cannon and the pointed arguments of muskets and bayonets. Because we refuse submission to the despotic power of a ministerial Parliament, our own sovereign, to whom we have been always ready to swear true allegiance,—whose authority we never meant to cast off, who might have continued happy in the cheerful obedience of as faithful subjects as any in his dominions,—has given us up to the rage of his ministers, to be seized at sea by the rapacious commanders of every little sloop of war and piratical cutter, and to be plundered and massacred by land by mercenary troops, who know no distinction betwixt an enemy and a brother, between right and wrong, but only, like brutal pursuers, to hunt and seize the prey pointed out by their masters.

We must keep our eyes fixed on the supreme government of the Eternal King, as directing all events, setting up or pulling down the kings of the earth at his pleasure, suffering the best forms of human government to degenerate and go to ruin by corruption, or restoring the decayed constitutions of kingdoms and states by reviving public virtue and religion, and granting the favorable interpositions of his providence. . . .[25]

Langdon's speech was duplicated literally thousands of times throughout the colonies both before and during the Revolutionary War. But one pastor in particular is credited by historians with presenting the biblical reasons for resistance to tyrants. His name was Reverend Jonathan Mayhew, a Harvard graduate and pastor of Boston's West Church. In January 1750, Mayhew delivered a sermon titled "A Discourse Concerning Unlimited Submission" that was soon reprinted and spread throughout the colonies. Mayhew argued powerfully against the view that Romans 13:1–3 requires Christians to submit to ungodly government authorities. Mayhew called it blasphemy "to call tyrants and oppressors God's ministers." In his sermon, Mayhew wrote:

What unprejudiced man can think that God made ALL to be thus subservient to the lawless pleasure and frenzy of ONE, so that it shall always be a sin to resist him! Nothing but the most plain and express revelation from heaven could make a sober impartial man believe such a monstrous, unaccountable doctrine, and, indeed, the thing itself appears so shocking—so out of all proportion, that it may be questioned whether all the miracles that ever were wrought could make it credible, that this doctrine really came from God. At present, there is not the least syllable of Scripture which gives any countenance to it.[26]

Pastors and Guns

Revolutionary War pastors not only preached on the biblical right to resist tyranny, but they also joined forces with the militias being formed to fight the British. Churches were fortified and were places where arms and powder were often stored. They were also refuges for the citizens to run to if the town was attacked.

In my work on Capitol Hill I frequently visit the Capitol building itself. The reminders of the men of God who battled to establish the republic stand out as reminders to me of how far the secularists have carried us from the intentions of the founders.

In the Small House Rotunda between the main Rotunda and the Old House Chamber stands the statue of Rev. John Peter Muhlenberg, who pastored two churches in Virginia in the early 1770s, one an English-speaking Episcopal church and the other a German-speaking Lutheran church. He was also a member of the Virginia legislature at the outbreak of the Revolutionary War. After the British seized Virginia's armory in Williamsburg, Pastor Muhlenberg forged a course of action. On January 21, 1776, he stood at his pulpit and delivered a message from Ecclesiastes: "To every thing there is a season, and a time to every purpose under the heaven" (v. 1, KJV). In that message he told his flock that the time was not one of peace, but of war. At the conclusion of his sermon he took off his clerical robe to reveal his uniform as an officer of the Revolution. Outside he rallied some three hundred men from his congregation that day to join him. This was the birth of the Eighth Virginia Regiment, which fought throughout the war, including the last battle at Yorktown, in which the British were defeated. At Yorktown he protected Washington's right flank with the First Brigade of Lafayette's Infantry. Without Pastor Muhlenberg the possibility exists that the British would have been victorious at Yorktown and the war lost. (This will be discussed further in chapter 5.) Reverend John Peter Muhlenberg is not the only preacher, nor the only Muhlenberg to be remembered in the art and statuary of the Capitol. His brother was Reverend Frederick Augustus Muhlenberg, a New York City pastor. Originally critical of his brother for joining the war effort, Frederick himself joined the revolutionary movement after the British invaded New York City. He was later elected to Congress and became a Speaker of the House, and it is for that reason that his portrait hangs in the Speaker's Lobby, just outside the House Chamber.

Officers in the Continental Army included pastors from the Baptist Church, the Episcopal Church, the Presbyterian Church, the German Reformed Church, and the Lutheran Church, and those are but the ones I have identified. Presbyterian clergy accounted for two generals and at least five colonels in Washington's army.

Clergy did not serve on the battlefield alone. Pastor Elisha Fish published a sermon titled "The Art of War Lawful and Necessary for a Christian People" that was widely distributed. Fish argued that free men bearing arms to defend liberty were the "true strength and safety of every commonwealth."

A month before the battle of Lexington and Concord, Rev. William Emerson preached to the Concord militia. During his sermon, he warned the British: "It will be your unspeakable Damage to meddle with us, for we have an unconquered Leader that carries his people to Victory and Triumph."[27] Five weeks later, the first man to muster at the North Bridge in Concord against the redcoats was Reverend Emerson! It was Reverend Emerson's grandson, Ralph Waldo Emerson (a transcendentalist and former Unitarian minister), who wrote the Concord Hymn commemorating this historic event in Lexington and Concord:

By the rude bridge that arched the flood
Their flag to April's breeze unfurled
Here once the embattled farmers stood
And fired the shot heard round the world

The foe long since in silence slept
Alike the Conqueror silent sleeps
And Time the ruined bridge has swept
Down the dark stream which seaward creeps

On this green bank, by this soft stream
We set to-day a votive stone
That memory may their deed redeem
When like our sires our sons are gone

Spirit! who made those freemen dare
To die, or leave their children free
Bid time and nature gently spare
The shaft we raise to them and Thee.[28]

The pastors of New England used their pulpits to teach the colonists about the right to resist tyranny and to encourage them to be willing to die to establish a new nation based upon religious freedom, limited government, and free speech! The Black Regiment of pastors can be credited with inflaming patriotic passions against British tyranny.

The historical record is clear: From the beginning of this nation, civil leaders and pastors alike believed that America was founded "under God" and that our nation had a special calling from God to fulfill in history.

Patrick Henry affirmed this truth when he wrote in March 1775: "It cannot be emphasized too strongly or too often that this great nation was founded, not by religionists, but by Christians; not on religions, but on the Gospel of Jesus Christ. For this very reason peoples of other faiths have been afforded asylum, prosperity, and freedom of worship here."[29]

CHAPTER 3

Background of the Pledge of Allegiance

T HE Pledge of Allegiance was published for the first time in the fall of 1892. However, in order to understand how and why the Pledge came to be written by Francis Bellamy, it is important to understand the historical events taking place during the decades prior to its creation.

The Pledge came out of a chaotic time in American history involving immigration reform, anarchists, Marxists, labor conflicts, and unrestricted economic growth in America.

Immigration was, for the most part, unrestricted until 1882, when Congress passed the Chinese Exclusion Act to place quotas on how many Chinese could enter the country. In 1892, Ellis Island was opened to process and screen the hundreds of thousands of immigrants who were arriving in America from Europe. The flood of immigrants during this period were from eastern Europe, and there was a growing fear in America that these immigrants were anarchists or Marxists who would subvert our way of life. There was also fear that because many of them were Jewish or Catholic, they would also undermine the overall "Protestant" culture that had existed in America since the Mayflower Compact.

Americans could see what was happening in Europe as revolutionary socialist and anarchist movements were spreading

41

from nation to nation. In addition, nineteenth-century Americans had also seen the horrors of anarchy in the Haymarket Riot in Chicago in 1886.

The Haymarket protest was organized by the Knights of Labor, a coalition of anarchists and socialists who demanded eight-hour workdays. They were protesting against the McCormack Harvesting Machine Company and began a strike May 1. During several days of striking and protesting, police came out to restore order. Someone threw a pipe bomb at the police, and seven officers died in the blast. More than sixty other policemen were injured. The police fired into the crowd, killing four.[1]

America was also rocked by the Homestead Strike of 1892. This pitted the Carnegie Steel Company against the Amalgamated Association of Iron and Steel Workers. A strike in 1889 by union organizers had won workers a three-year contract, but Carnegie was determined to break the union and locked workers out of the plant after they refused to work longer hours. Three hundred Pinkerton men were called by Carnegie's plant manager, Henry Frick, but the Pinkertons met 10,000 strikers. During the battle, seven Pinkerton guards were killed and nine strikers died. The militia was called in to protect strikebreakers and the plant was reopened. The strike created sympathy for the workers, but when anarchist Alexander Berkman tried to kill Frick, support for the strikers evaporated, and the fear of anarchy in America grew.[2]

Americans not only feared the influx of eastern European anarchists and socialists into America, but they also feared that the new wave of immigrants would bring strange religious practices to these shores. A poem written by Thomas Bailey Aldrich in 1892 and published in the *Atlantic Monthly* expressed this sentiment:

Wide open and unguarded stand our gates,
And through them presses a wild motley throng—
Men from the Volga and the Tartar steppes,

Featureless figures of the Hoang-Ho,
Malayan, Scythian, Teuton, Kelt, and Slav,
Flying the Old World's poverty and scorn;
These bringing with them unknown gods and rites,
Those, tiger passions, here to stretch their claws . . .[3]

Another fear that Americans had about eastern European immigrants was that they would not assimilate into American culture, learn our language, or appreciate our political system and its benefits.

Nineteenth-century Americans understood that immigrants who failed to assimilate into the culture would be ripe for exploitation by radical socialists and anarchists who were infiltrating labor movements and political parties. Communist and anarchist organizations and newspapers printed in non-English languages began to spring up in the larger cities—and this threatened the American way of life.

Not only were Americans in the late nineteenth century worried about anarchists and Communists, but there was also growing concern about the increasing numbers of Mafia immigrants coming into the United States from Sicily and mainland Italy to set up crime syndicates in America's major cities.

The year 1892 was a particularly busy year for the immigration of mafiosi into New York. Three key Mafia leaders arrived in New York that year to set up criminal operations. The Provenzano crime family fled from New York to New Orleans after losing a power struggle in the Big Apple with another organization. New Orleans then became a haven for criminal enterprises. In 1895, a Mafia organization was established in Chicago. Little wonder the infiltration of anarchists, Communists, and Mafia criminals into our culture was such an alarming social trend to Americans.

Americans knew the history of Europe and were aware that the European continent had been shaken by forty-eight revolutions in the previous fifty years. In addition, after having gone through the horrors of the Civil War only thirty years before, the American citizens in 1892 wanted to make sure new immigrants would learn to appreciate political freedom and the benefits of constitutional government.

The immigrants needed to be integrated into American culture and learn to appreciate its ideals of limited government, free speech, and freedom of religion.

The Pledge's Christian Socialist Author

Not only was 1892 the year Ellis Island opened and the Homestead Strike occurred, but it was also the 400th anniversary of the discovery of America by Christopher Columbus. This anniversary was of great interest to the Knights of Columbus (K of C), a Catholic charitable group that had been formed in 1882. The Knights of Columbus was organized by Father Michael J. McGivney as a service group to help Catholics and to help Catholic immigrants fully integrate into American society. The members of the K of C were dedicated to be defenders of America, their families, and their faith. They named their new organization after Christopher Columbus, for his role in bringing Christianity to the New World in 1492.[4]

Naturally, the Knights of Columbus wanted to take a key leadership role in celebrating the 400th anniversary of the discovery of America. As part of their effort, they lobbied Congress to make Columbus Day a national celebration with patriotic festivals all over the United States and especially for public school children.

President Benjamin Harrison approved of the K of C plan, and Francis Bellamy, a former Baptist pastor, was picked to plan a series of national events for public school children. Included in this Columbus Day celebration was the recitation for the first time of the Pledge of Allegiance!

The history of the Pledge of Allegiance is fascinating because Francis Bellamy, the author of the Pledge, actually had written it not necessarily to promote American patriotism, but to be used internationally as a pledge of loyalty to governments. Over the years, however, due to the lobbying work of the Knights of Columbus and other patriotic groups, the Pledge came to be a statement of allegiance to the United States and its principles of justice and religious freedom, and its existence as a nation "under God."

Francis Bellamy graduated from Rochester Theological Seminary in 1880 and became pastor of the Dearborn Street Baptist Church in Boston in 1885. In 1889, the Society of Christian Socialists was formed in Boston and Francis Bellamy became the head of the education section of the group.[5]

Bellamy's Socialist ideas were also reflected in the writings of his cousin Edward Bellamy, known for the second-best-selling book of the time called *Looking Backward*. The utopian novel describes a man who travels into the future to the year 2000 in America and finds that our nation has become a Socialist paradise. The book was published in 1887 and outsold every other book except *Uncle Tom's Cabin* at the time.

In 1891, Francis Bellamy became a leading spokesman of the First Nationalist Club, a Socialist group devoted to implementing the ideals expressed in *Looking Backward*. The First Nationalist Club was actually part of a network of Socialist groups associated with the British Fabian Socialist Society, established in 1889. The Fabians favored the gradual imposition of Socialism upon countries through propaganda and political action, not violent revolution as advocated by their Marxist allies. One of the Fabian symbols was the tortoise, symbolizing patient gradualism in converting nations to Socialism. The other Fabian symbol was a wolf in sheep's clothing— indicating the willingness of Socialists to use deceit to achieve their goals.

Pastor Bellamy resigned from Dearborn Street Baptist Church after realizing that his Socialist views were too radical for his congregation at the time. He was then hired as a staff member of *The Youth's Companion*, a well-respected youth culture magazine of the day.

Shortly after joining *The Youth's Companion*, Bellamy was asked to take charge of plans for the upcoming Columbus Day celebration to be held on October 12. In February 1892, Bellamy presented his Columbus Day plan to the National Association of School Superintendents, and the head of this group then asked Bellamy to head up the Columbus Day celebration for the National Education Association.

In March of that year, Bellamy published a note to public school officials in *The Youth's Companion* urging schools all over America to host Columbus Day celebrations. He told them: "It is for you, scholars of the American Public Schools, to arouse a sentiment in your schools and in your neighborhoods for this grand way of celebrating the Finding of America. Educators and teachers will meet you from their side. But it is for you to begin. . . . The Public School of today sways the hundred years to come."

As part of this Columbus Day celebration, *The Youth's Companion* distributed flag ceremony information and merchandise. The magazine also offered students the gift of a beautiful medal if they could initiate a flag ceremony in their school before Columbus Day. By September 1892, more than 26,000 schools had ordered flags and instructions for carrying out flag ceremonies. Bellamy also sent out announcements to ministers around the country asking that they preach sermons on the relationship of a free public school education to American life before summer recess in 1892.[6]

Included in this effort to celebrate Columbus Day was a Pledge of Allegiance written by Bellamy. This Pledge was to be recited by students during their celebration of Columbus Day.

The Pledge was published for the first time in the September 8, 1892, issue of *The Youth's Companion*:

I pledge allegiance to my Flag,
and the Republic for which it
stands:
one Nation indivisible,
with Liberty and Justice for all.

A month earlier, Bellamy had described his thoughts on writing the Pledge:

It began as an intensive communing with salient points of our national history, from the Declaration of Independence onwards; with the makings of the Constitution . . . with the meaning of the Civil War; with the aspiration of the people . . .

The true reason for allegiance to the Flag is the "Republic for which it stands". . . . And what does that vast thing, the Republic mean? It is the concise political word for the Nation—the one nation which the Civil War was fought to prove. To make that "one nation" idea clear, we must specify that it is indivisible, as Webster and Lincoln used to repeat in their great speeches. And its future?

Just here arose the temptation of the historic slogan of the French Revolution which meant so much to Jefferson and his friends, "Liberty, equality, fraternity." No, that would be too fanciful, too many thousands of years off in realization. But we as a nation do stand square on the doctrine of liberty and justice for all . . .[7]

Historian John W. Baer, author of *The Pledge of Allegiance: A Centennial History 1892–1992*, says that Bellamy's lack of reference in the Pledge to the *American* flag was no accident.

According to Baer, "Bellamy wanted it as an international peace pledge, so he hoped that all the republics [of the world] . . . on their peace day, would put a white border around their flag, and recite it as a pledge."[8]

Regardless of the Socialist origins of the Pledge of Allegiance, the 1892 Columbus Day celebration was an amazing success for the marketing abilities of Bellamy and *The Youth's Companion*. It has been estimated that on Columbus Day 1892, more than twelve million children stood in their classrooms, faced the American flag, and recited the Pledge of Allegiance! The original instructions for saying the Pledge included the following recommendations:

> At a signal from the Principal, the pupils, in ordered ranks, hands to the side, face the Flag. Another signal is given; every pupil gives the military salute—right hand lifted, palm downward, to a line with the forehead and close to it. Standing thus, all repeat together, slowly: "I pledge allegiance to my Flag and the Republic for which it stands: one Nation indivisible, with Liberty and Justice for All." At the words, "to my Flag," the right hand is extended gracefully, palm upwards, towards the Flag, and remains in this gesture till the end of the affirmation; whereupon all hands immediately drop to the side. Then, still standing, as the instruments strike a chord, all will sing AMERICA—"My Country, 'Tis of Thee."[9]

(The use of the extended hand salute, known as the Roman salute, fell out of favor in the United States during the early years of World War II with the rise of Fascism in Italy and Nazism in Germany.)

In 1954, as the Senate and the House were both debating resolutions to add "under God" to the Pledge, one senator said he had received from Francis Bellamy's son a copy of his father's description of how he wrote the pledge. To provide historical context to the congressional debate over adding "under God," the senator entered into the *Congressional Record* (June 7, 1954) Bellamy's description of his role in writing the Pledge of Allegiance:

> At the beginning of the nineties patriotism and national feeling was at a low ebb. The patriotic ardor of the Civil War was an old story. The country was then in a period of dazzling prosperity and the chase for what was called the nimble dollar was most in people's minds. The time was ripe for a reawakening of Simple Americanism and the leaders in the new movement rightly felt that patriotic education should begin in the public schools.
>
> I was at that time with the Youth's Companion, of Boston, doing work with James B. Upham, a member of the firm. Mr. Upham felt that a flag should be on every schoolhouse. The Youth's Companion fostered a plan of selling flags to schools through the children themselves, at cost, which was so successful that 25,000 schools acquired flags in one year.
>
> Mr. Upham also had a greater scheme, the result of which was that every school in the land on a certain day would have a flag raising, under most impressive conditions. The day was to be Columbus Day, 1892—the 400th anniversary of the discovery of America. Mr. Upham declared that that day should mark a new consecration of patriotism and to that end conceived the National Columbian celebration. I was made chairman of the executive committee for that work and immediately began to enlist the support of not only the superintendents of education in all the States, but also worked with Governors, Congressmen, even the President of the United States. The result was a universal holiday declared for Columbus Day, 1892, by proclamation of Benjamin Harrison.

Of course there had to be an official program for universal use in all the schools. It had to be more than a list of exercises. The ritual must be prepared with simplicity and dignity. An ode, rich in feeling and diction, was written by Edna Dean Proctor. There was also an oration suitable for declamation.

Of course the nub of the program was to be the raising of the flag, with a salute to the flag recited by the pupils in unison. That was the rub. There was not a satisfactory enough form for this salute. The Balch salute, which ran—

I give my heart and my hand to my country—One country, one language, one flag—seemed too juvenile and lacking in dignity. Mr. Upham and I spent many hours in considering the revision of this salute. Each one suggested that the other write a new salute. It was my thought that a vow of loyalty or allegiance to the flag should be the dominant idea. I especially stressed the word "allegiance." So Mr. Upham told me to try it out on that line.

It was on a warm evening in August 1892, in my office in Boston, that I shut myself in my room alone to formulate the actual pledge. Beginning with the new word "allegiance," I first decided that "pledge" was a better school word than "vow" or "swear"; and that the first person singular should be used, and that "my" flag was preferable to "the."

When those first words "I pledge allegiance to my flag" looked up at me from the scratch paper, the start appeared promising. Then for the further reach: should it be "country," "Nation," or "Republic"? That was hard. "Republic" won because it distinguished the form of government chosen by the fathers and established by the Revolution. The true reason for allegiance to the flag is the "Republic for which it stands."

Now how should the vista be widened so as to teach the national fundamentals? I laid down my pencil and tried to pass our history in review. It took in the sayings of Washington, the arguments of Hamilton, the Webster-Hayne debate, the speeches of Seward and Lincoln, the Civil War. After many attempts all that pictured struggle reduced itself to three words, "One Nation, indivisible." To reach that compact brevity, conveying the facts of a single nationality and of an indivisibility of States and of common interests, was, as I recall, the most arduous phase of the task, and the discarded experiments at phrasing overflowed the scrap basket.

But what of the present and future of this indivisible Nation here presented for allegiance? What were the old and fought-out issues which always will be issues to be fought for? Especially, what were the basic national doctrines bearing upon the acute questions already agitating the public mind? Here was a temptation to repeat the historic slogan of the French Revolution, imported by Jefferson, "liberty, fraternity, equality." But that was rather quickly rejected, as fraternity was too remote of realization, and as equality was a dubious word. What doctrines, then, would everybody agree upon as the basis of Americanism? "Liberty and justice" were surely basic, were undebatable, and were all that any one Nation could handle. If they were exercised for all they involved the spirit of equality and fraternity. So that final line came with a cheering rush. As a clincher it seemed to assemble the past and to promise the future.

That, I remember, is how the sequence of the ideas grew and how the words were found, on that August night with the cooling Boston sea breeze coming into the window.

I called for Mr. Upham and repeated it to him with full emphasis. He liked it. His colleagues in the Youth's

Companion also approved of it and it was printed in the official program.

That is the story of how these famous 23 words came to be written. In later years the word [*sic*] "to my flag" were changed to "to the flag of the United States of America" because of the large number of foreign children in the schools. This enlargement was probably done with good reason, but it did injure the rhythmic balance of the original composition.[10]

The Pledge Becomes a Daily Routine

After the 1892 Columbus Day celebration, the recitation of the Pledge of Allegiance became a routine part of the day for public school children throughout America. In 1898, the day after the United States declared war on Spain, the New York legislature passed the first "flag salute statute," mandating the daily flag salute in all New York schools. The law stated:

> It shall be the duty of the state superintendent of public instruction to prepare, for the use of the public schools of the state, a program for a salute to the flag at the opening of each day of school, and such other patriotic exercises as may be deemed by him to be expedient, under such regulations and instructions as may best meet the varied needs of the different grades in such schools.[11]

Similar statutes were passed by Rhode Island in 1901, Arizona in 1903, Kansas in 1907, and Maryland in 1918.

Political Turmoil Spurs Action on Pledge

The Pledge of Allegiance remained unchanged until 1924, when the National Flag Conference under the sponsorship of the

American Legion and Daughters of the American Revolution lobbied to change the words "my Flag" in the Pledge to "the Flag of the United States of America."

The change was made because both of these patriotic groups felt the Pledge should be more specifically American in its tone—rather than simply being a pledge to any flag. This effort was fueled by the radical activities of anarchists and Marxists in the United States and around the world who were pushing for revolution. Patriotic groups were also concerned about assimilating new immigrants and helping them learn to appreciate America's political freedoms under the Constitution. Having immigrant children pledge their allegiance to the American flag and to our republican form of government was one way of helping immigrants learn what it meant to be an American.

The early 1900s were characterized by radical leftist and anarchist activities. President William McKinley was shot September 6, 1901, by an anarchist named Leon Czolgosz. McKinley died on September 14.[12]

The 1900s also saw the continuing rise of leftist agitation within labor unions, with violence usually following such efforts. In 1905, the radical Industrial Workers of the World (IWW) was organized in Chicago and began agitating workers. A year later, Emma Goldman launched the anarchist journal, *Mother Earth*.

Anarchist violence was on the upswing in 1905 with the murder of Idaho Governor Frank Steunenberg for his role in fighting radical union activities in Coeur d'Alene. The governor was killed by a bomb that had been rigged to explode when he opened the gate to his home. The killer was an anarchist named Harry Orchard, who admitted he'd been involved in numerous other murder attempts and railroad bombings.[13] And, in 1908, the Socialist Party's "Red Special Campaign Train" left Chicago to begin a promotional campaign on behalf of the Socialist candidate for president, Eugene V. Debs.

America continued to face numerous attacks from Socialist and anarchist organizations determined to undermine the country's system of government into the 1920s. This political climate provides context for an understanding of the motivation of the American Legion and Daughters of the American Revolution lobbying to add "the flag of the United States of America" to the Pledge. The American Legion and DAR were also concerned that immigrant children might think they were pledging allegiance to the flag of their home country, not the American flag. Francis Bellamy didn't want this change, but his protests were ignored.

Pledge Unchanged until 1954

In 1946, just one year after the end of World War II, Winston Churchill gave a chilling speech in Missouri about the growing darkness of Communist totalitarianism spreading in Europe. Churchill warned that, "an iron curtain has descended across the Continent. . . . The Communist parties, which were very small in all these Eastern States of Europe have been raised to pre-eminence and power far beyond their numbers and are seeking everywhere to obtain totalitarian control. Police governments are prevailing in nearly every case, and so far, except in Czechoslovakia, there is no true democracy."[14]

This speech is considered to be the beginning of the cold war era. American soldiers soon learned about Communist tyranny in the Korean War (1951–1953). They fought the North Korean Communists and the Red Chinese in our nation's first of two major "no-win" wars (Vietnam being the second one).

During the early 1950s, Senator Joseph McCarthy began holding hearings on the infiltration of Communists into the highest levels of our government. In my opinion, he has been unfairly and mercilessly smeared for his effort to protect our nation from Communist subversion. (Ann Coulter's book, *Treason: Liberal*

Treachery from the Cold War to the War on Terrorism, documents the history of the unfair attacks against McCarthy and others who were rightfully concerned about Communist subversion within our government during and after World War II.)

It was during this period of history—and because of concern over domestic Communist subversion and worry about the Soviet empire's efforts to conquer the world—that the patriotic Knights of Columbus began lobbying for a change in the Pledge of Allegiance. They began their effort to have "under God" added to the Pledge in 1953. Realizing that millions of children recited this Pledge each day in schools, it was important for these kids to realize that the American system of government was drastically different from Communist dictatorships that were based upon militant atheism and the glorification of state power. Under Communist regimes, the state was "god," not the one true God. Under Communist tyranny, anyone believing in God or not absolutely loyal to the all-powerful state could be imprisoned, tortured, and killed for his or her faith.

The Knights of Columbus rightly believed that American children needed an extra bit of education on the godly foundations of our nation—even if only through those two words, "under God," added to the Pledge.

Fifteen resolutions were offered in Congress to have "under God" added to the Pledge, but all failed. All this stonewalling changed, however, in 1954, thanks to a Sunday morning sermon given by the Scottish Rev. George Docherty at New York Presbyterian Church in Washington, D.C., February 4, 1954.

At ninety-one years of age, Reverend Docherty gave an interview to *Insight* magazine (July 29, 2002) on his role in getting "under God" added to the Pledge of Allegiance. He told the magazine reporter he wrote his sermon after learning about the Pledge from his son, who told him he recited the Pledge daily in his second-grade class. Docherty, who had immigrated from Scotland in 1950, had never heard of the Pledge until that moment.[15]

After delivering his homily on the Pledge, he asked one of his parishioners if he had enjoyed the sermon. That parishioner was President Dwight D. Eisenhower, who had been sitting in the front pew. Eisenhower told Docherty that he agreed with his sentiments about adding "under God" to the Pledge. Reverend Docherty's sermon became national news and within weeks, Senator Homer Ferguson (R-MI) sponsored a bill to add "under God" to the Pledge. It was approved as a Joint Resolution on June 8, 1954. President Eisenhower signed it into law on Flag Day, June 14. In his statement, Eisenhower said: "From this day forward, the millions of our school children will daily proclaim in every city and town, every village and rural schoolhouse, the dedication of our nation and our people to the Almighty."

Because Reverend Docherty's Pledge of Allegiance sermon is an important part of American history, I am reprinting portions of it below:

> Freedom is a subject everyone seems to be talking about without seemingly stopping to ask the rather basic question, "What do we mean by freedom?" In this matter, apparently, we are all experts. . . .
>
> Lincoln, in his day, saw this country as a nation that "was conceived in liberty and dedicated to the proposition that all men are created equal." And the question he asks is the timeless, and timely, one—"whether that Nation, or any Nation so conceived and so dedicated, can long endure."
>
> I recall once discussing the "American way of life" with a newspaper editor. He had been using the phrase rather freely. When asked to define the phrase "the American way of life," he became very wordy and verbose. "It is to live and let live; it is being free to act," and other such platitudes.

Let me tell you what "the American way of life" is. It is going to the ball game and eating popcorn, and drinking Coca Cola, and rooting for the Senators. It is shopping in Sears, Roebuck. It is losing heart and hat on a roller coaster. It is driving on the right side of the road and putting up at motels on a long journey. It is being bored with television commercials. It is setting off firecrackers with your children on the Fourth of July. It is sitting for seven hours to see the pageantry of the Presidential Inauguration.

But, it is deeper than that. . . .

And where did all this come from?

It has been with us so long, we have to recall it was brought here by people who laid stress on fundamentals . . .

These fundamental concepts of life had been given to the world from Sinai, where the moral law was graven upon tables of stone, symbolizing the universal application to all men; and they came from the New Testament, where they heard in the words of Jesus of Nazareth the living Word of God for the world. . . .

Now, all this may seem obvious until one sits down and takes these complications of freedom really seriously. For me, it came in a flash one day some time ago when our children came home from school. Almost casually, I asked what happened at school when they arrived there in the morning. They described to me, in great detail and with strange solemnity, the ritual of the salute to the flag. The children turn to the flag, and with their hand across their heart, they repeat the words: "I pledge allegiance to the flag of the United States of America, and to the Republic for which it stands, one nation, indivisible, with liberty and justice for all."

They were very proud of the pledge, and rightly so. . . .

I don't suppose you fathers would have paid much attention to that as I did . . . But I could sit down and brood upon it, going over each word slowly in my mind. And I came to a strange conclusion. There was something missing in this pledge, and that which was missing was the characteristic and definitive factor in the American way of life. In fact, I could hear little Muscovites repeat a similar pledge to their hammer-and-sickle flag in Moscow with equal solemnity, for Russia is also a republic that claims to have overthrown the tyranny of kingship. . . .

What, therefore, is missing in the Pledge of Allegiance that Americans have been saying off and on since 1892, and officially since 1942? The one fundamental concept that completely and ultimately separates Communist Russia from the democratic institutions of this country. . . .

We face, today, a theological war . . . It is a fight for freedom of the human personality. It is not simply man's inhumanity to man. It is Armageddon, a battle of the gods. It is the view of man as it comes down to us from Judeo-Christian civilization in mortal combat against modern, secularized, godless humanity.

The Pledge of Allegiance seems to me to omit this theological implication that is fundamental to the American way of life. It should be "one nation, indivisible, under God." Once "under God," then we can define what we mean by "liberty and justice for all." To omit the words "under God" in the Pledge of Allegiance is to omit the definitive character of the American way of life.

Some might assert this to be a violation of the First Amendment to the Constitution. It is quite the opposite. The First Amendment states concerning the question of religion: "Congress shall make no law respecting the establishment of religion."

Now, "establishment of religion" is a technical term. It means Congress will permit no state church in this land such as exists in England. In England the bishops are appointed by Her Majesty. The church, by law, is supported to teinds [tithe for the clergy] or rents. The church, therefore, can call upon the support of the law of the land to carry out its own ecclesiastical laws. What the declaration says, in effect, is that no state church shall exist in this land. This is a separation of church and state; it is not, and never was meant to be, a separation of religion and life. Such objection is a confusion of the First Amendment with the First Commandment.

If we were to use the phrase "under the church," that would be different. In fact, it would be dangerous. The question arises, which church? Now, I can give good Methodists an excellent dissertation upon the virtues of the Presbyterian Church, and show how much superior John Knox was to John Wesley. But the whole sad story of church history shows how, of all tyrants, often the church could be the worst for the best of reasons. The Jewish Church persecuted unto death the Christian Church in the first decade of Christianity; and for 1,200 years the Christian Church persecuted the Jewish Church. The Roman Church persecuted the Protestants; and the Protestants, in turn, persecuted the Roman Church; the Presbyterians and the Episcopalians brought low the very name of Christian charity, both in Scotland and America. It is not for nothing that Thomas Jefferson, on his tombstone at Monticello, claimed that one of the three achievements of his life was his fight for religious freedom in Virginia—that even above the exalted office of President of the United States. No church is infallible; and no churchman is infallible.

Of course, as Christians, we might include the words "under Jesus Christ" or "under the King of Kings." But one of the glories of this land is that it had opened its gates to all men of every religious faith. . . .

There is no religious examination on entering the United States of America—no persecution because a man's faith differs even from the Christian religion. So, it must be "under God," to include the great Jewish community, and the people of Moslem faith, and the myriad of *denominations* of Christians in the land.

What then of the honest atheist?

Philosophically speaking, an atheistic American is a contradiction in terms. Now don't misunderstand me. This age has thrown up a new type of man—call him secular; he does not believe in God; not because he is a wicked man, but because he is dialectically honest, and would rather walk with the unbelievers than sit hypocritically with people of the faith. These men, and many have I known, are fine in character; and in the obligations as citizens and good neighbors, quite excellent.

But they really are spiritual parasites. And I mean no term of abuse in this. I'm simply classifying them. A parasite is an organism that lives upon the life force of another organism without contributing to the life of the other. These excellent ethical seculars are living upon the accumulated spiritual capital of Judeo-Christian civilization, and at the same time, deny the God who revealed the divine principles upon which the ethics of this country grow. The dilemma of the secular is quite simple.

He cannot deny the Christian revelation and logically live the Christian ethic. And if he denies the Christian ethic, he falls short of the American ideal of life.

In Jefferson's phrase, if we deny the existence of the God who gave us life, how can we live by the liberty He gave us at the same time? This is a God-fearing nation. On our coins, bearing the imprint of Lincoln and Jefferson, are the words "In God we trust."

Congress is opened with prayer. It is upon the Holy Bible the President takes his oath of office. Naturalized citizens, when they take their oath of allegiance, conclude, solemnly, with the words "so help me God."

In this land, there is neither Jew nor Greek, neither bond nor free; neither male nor female, for we are one nation indivisible under God, and humbly as God has given us the light we seek liberty and justice for all. This quest is not only within these United States, but to the four corners of the globe, wherever man will lift up his head toward the vision of his true and divine manhood.[16]

Reverend Docherty's eloquent speech should be read in every school across this nation and by liberal judges who either willingly or naively misinterpret the First Amendment as meaning that "under God" is an unconstitutional statement in our Pledge. In reading his sermon, I was struck by his comment about atheists as parasites who live off the benefits of our Judeo-Christian heritage yet contribute nothing to our rich heritage of freedom. Reverend Docherty's perspective on atheists is timely in view of the efforts by atheist Michael Newdow to strip the Pledge of "under God" and to remove "In God We Trust" from our coins and paper currency. Newdow's atheism is appropriately called parasitism for it sucks the life from a host—America's Christian heritage—and gives nothing in return.

Adding "under God" to the Pledge of Allegiance was in no way out of the ordinary for the Congress, even as late as 1954. That same year the Congressional Prayer Chapel was opened for use by members of the House and Senate. In the front of the chapel is a stained glass window that portrays George Washington kneeling in prayer. Above Washington the words "This nation under God" are inscribed. Surrounding his portrait is Psalm 16:1: "Preserve me, O God, for in thee do I put my trust." While the chapel is for the use of members only, the actual House Chambers were used for church services through much of the nineteenth century.

CHAPTER **4**

Challenges to the Pledge

T HE federal courts, including the Supreme Court, have shown they are incapable of issuing constitutionally sound rulings on freedom of religion. They are blinded by their own ideologies and are deliberately hamstrung by a history of wrongly decided rulings and misinterpretations of what the Constitution and the Founding Fathers really meant about the separation of church and state. The federal courts have built a complicated maze of contradictory decisions—all based upon the "precedent" of previously decided wrong rulings. The result is the incredibly convoluted legal quagmire we face today.

The history of the Pledge of Allegiance is, unfortunately, a testimony to the unrestricted power of judges who believe they have the authority to redefine the Constitution and to erase our nation's Christian roots.

A Brief Review of Legal Cases

Challenges to the recitation of the Pledge of Allegiance were relatively few during the decades leading up to the late 1930s. Most Americans were patriotic and had no problem with their children pledging allegiance to the American flag and to the Republic.

A change began to occur, however, in the late 1930s, and it involved Jehovah's Witness children who objected to saying the Pledge because their faith forbade them from having "false idols" before God. Pledging allegiance to a flag or the United States was considered a sin to them. The first reported challenge to saying the Pledge of Allegiance in school was in 1937 in the case of *Nichols v. Mayor of Lynn (Massachusetts).* The Supreme Judicial Court of Massachusetts rejected a Jehovah's Witness challenge to reciting the Pledge based upon the First Amendment's protection of free speech. The court said that saying the pledge was a valid legislative enactment and did not establish a penalty for a disobedient student who refused to say it. The court said the state had the right "to inculcate patriotism and to instill recognition of the blessings conferred by orderly government."[1] The court also said that the Pledge did not restrain anyone from worshipping God under the First Amendment.

In another 1937 case, *Leoles v. Landers,* the U.S. Supreme Court dismissed an appeal from Georgia in a case involving a student who refused to recite the Pledge. A state court sided with school officials and ruled they had acted lawfully when they expelled students who refused to salute the flag. The state court asserted that the school officials were simply doing their duty in instructing children on devotion to America and its ideals.[2]

A year later, in the case of *Hering v. State Board of Education,* the U.S. Supreme Court dismissed an appeal from New Jersey, where the state court had ruled that a student could be required to say the Pledge because it wasn't an oath.

In 1939, in the case of *Johnson v. Town of Deerfield,* the U.S. Supreme Court affirmed a lower federal court ruling in Massachusetts in favor of a state regulation requiring students to recite the oath. On the same day, the California State Supreme Court ruled in *Gabrielli v. Knickerbocker* that a local school board had the power to impose reasonable regulations on students designed to promote good citizenship, patriotism, and loyalty to the state and nation. In the *Gabrielli* case, the Supreme Court of California ruled:

> The legislature has conferred upon school boards broad plenary powers to make all reasonable regulations that will in the reasonable exercise of judgment promote the efficiency of the school system in performing public welfare duties, which are limited not merely to the development of the mind in academic fields, but the sphere of which is much broader and extends to those subjects which will tend to {Page 12 Cal.2d 92} develop and quicken the civic conscience in ways of attachment for home and country.{7} It is only where its regulations are clearly shown to be in violation of the fundamental law that the courts, even though entertaining a different opinion from that of the governing boards as to the wisdom or expediency of adopting social regulations, may annul them. Many authorities may be cited sustaining the action of school boards in matters in which the wisdom of the board's action may be so highly controversial that reasonable minds might well be divided as to the wisdom of the board's action. In such cases, its action is conclusive.{8} We see no violation of any article of the federal or state Constitutions in its exercise of power in the instant case. The training of school children in good citizenship, patriotism and loyalty to state and nation is regarded by the law of the state as a means of protecting public welfare and is directed by the school code of the state. (Sec. 5.544.) The simple salutation to the flag and the repetition of the pledge of allegiance, in the judgment of the proper governing body, tend to stimulate in the minds of youth in the formative period of life sentiments of lasting affection and respect for and unfaltering loyalty to our government and its institutions. The judgment is reversed and the writ is discharged.[3]

The Supreme Court Reverses Itself

As these cases were decided, a shift began to occur in the U.S. Supreme Court's view of the right of schools to require students to recite the Pledge. The case that eventually led to two key Supreme Court decisions on requiring students to say the Pledge involved a third-grade student named Carleton Nicholls, Jr. As a devout Jehovah's Witness, he refused to say the Pledge in his Lynn, Massachusetts, classroom in late 1935. As a result, he was expelled from school. His expulsion became a major concern for the leaders of the Jehovah's Witnesses, and one of the officials of the church went on the radio to protest the expulsion of Nicholls for his religious beliefs.[4] In Minersville, Pennsylvania, two other Jehovah's Witness children heard about the Nicholls case and decided to stop reciting the Pledge, too. Lillian (age twelve) and Billy Gobitas (age ten) both refused to say the Pledge and were removed from the class. On November 5, 1935, Billy wrote a letter to the school board explaining his reasons for refusing to recite the Pledge. His parents decided to homeschool both children, but the school board opposed the decision and threatened to send the children to a reform school.

In May 1937, Lillian and Billy's father, William, filed a complaint with a federal district court in Philadelphia claiming that requiring his children to recite the Pledge violated their religious beliefs and denied them their "rights and privileges" under the Constitution. In June 1938, the federal court sided with Gobitas and ruled that the school had denied these children due process under the Fourteenth Amendment to the Constitution.[5] Undeterred, the Minersville school board appealed this decision with an appellate court but lost again.

The Minersville school board then filed yet another appeal—this time to the U.S. Supreme Court. In April 1940, the Supreme Court heard arguments from both sides on this issue. Chief Justice Charles Evans Hughes sided with the parents, but Justice Felix Frankfurter sided with the school board. Frankfurter, who emigrated from Europe as a child, said he believed that public schools had a responsibility to instill love of America in the children of immigrants.

In June 1940, the Supreme Court issued an 8–1 decision in favor of the school district, reversing the two lower-court decisions. Frankfurter wrote in this opinion, "National unity is the basis of national security," and that society may "utilize the educational process for inculcating those almost unconscious feelings which bind men together in a comprehending loyalty."[6] (Note: Justice Frankfurter's comments are especially relevant today in light of our nation's war on Islamic terrorism around the globe. He is correct in saying that national unity is the basis of national security. A nation divided as it was during the Vietnam War will be ineffective in defending our freedoms from aggressive and merciless enemies. It is important for our institutions— including schools—to support patriotism.)

The case under consideration was *Minersville School District v. Gobitis*, decided June 3, 1940. (A federal clerk had misspelled Gobitas, but the misspelling has remained in federal documents.)

Frankfurter went on to assert that the state had the right to "awaken in the child's mind considerations as to the significance of the flag contrary to those implanted by the parent" so long as the parents still remained free to "counteract by their own persuasiveness the wisdom and rightness of those loyalties which the state's educational system is seeking to promote."[7] In essence, Frankfurter was arguing that it was the right of the state to teach school children values that might be contrary to those of the parents—as long as the parents remained free to teach the opposite values at home. (Frankfurter's belief that schools should be free to teach values that oppose the values of parents is a controversial topic that cannot be discussed adequately in this book.)

Justice Harlan Fisk Stone wrote a dissenting opinion in the *Minersville* case that actually became the dominant Supreme

Court viewpoint just three years later when the Court *reversed* its own decision and overturned the 1940 *Gobitis* decision. In Stone's 1940 dissenting opinion he wrote:

> The law which is thus sustained is unique in the history of Anglo-American legislation. It does more than suppress freedom of speech and more than prohibit the free exercise of religion, which concededly are forbidden by the First Amendment and are violations of the liberty guaranteed by the Fourteenth. For by this law the state seeks to coerce these children to express a sentiment which, as they interpret it, they do not entertain, and which violates their deepest religious convictions. It is not denied that such compulsion is a prohibited infringement of personal liberty, freedom of speech and religion, guaranteed by the Bill of Rights, except in so far as it may be justified and supported as a proper exercise of the state's power over public education. Since the state, [310 U.S. 586, 602] in competition with parents, may through teaching in the public schools indoctrinate the minds of the young, it is said that in aid of its undertaking to inspire loyalty and devotion to constituted authority and the flag which symbolizes it, it may coerce the pupil to make affirmation contrary to his belief and in violation of his religious faith. And, finally, it is said that since the Minersville School Board and others are of the opinion that the country will be better served by conformity than by the observance of religious liberty which the Constitution prescribes, the courts are not free to pass judgment on the Board's choice.[8]

After the *Gobitis* decision was issued, Jehovah's Witness children were expelled from schools in at least 38 states for refusing to recite the Pledge. The supreme courts of Kansas and Washington expressed hostility toward the *Gobitis* decision and used their religious-liberty provisions in state constitutions to strike down flag-salute requirements.[9]

In March 1943, the Supreme Court issued a ruling in *West Virginia State Board of Education v. Barnette*. This case was almost identical to the *Gobitis* case from 1940. A school district had expelled three Jehovah's Witness students for refusing to recite the Pledge, but a federal court had ordered them back to school, and the school district appealed the case to the Supreme Court.[10] In the 1943 *West Virginia* decision, the Court reversed its *Gobitis* ruling from 1940 and sided with the children and parents. The Court's majority decision concluded with this statement:

> If there is any fixed star in our constitutional constellation, it is that no official, high or petty, can prescribe what shall be orthodox in politics, nationalism, religion, or other matters of opinion or force citizens to confess by word or act their faith therein. If there are any circumstances which permit an exception, they do not now occur to us.
>
> We think the action of the local authorities in compelling the flag salute and pledge transcends constitutional limitations on their power and invades the sphere of intellect and spirit which it is the purpose of the First Amendment to our Constitution to reserve from all official control.
>
> The decision of this Court in *Minersville School District v. Gobitis* and the holdings of those few per curiam decisions which preceded and foreshadowed it are overruled, and the judgment enjoining enforcement of the West Virginia Regulation is affirmed.[11]

Thus, in just three years, the Supreme Court had reversed itself on a key religious freedom case, thus proving that the concept of "precedent" as settled law in Supreme Court decisions isn't as sacred as liberals would have us believe. Perhaps precedent isn't really as firmly embedded in such cases as *Roe v. Wade* or *Lawrence v. Texas* as liberals wish.

The Pledge was not challenged again until 1966, in a case involving Black Muslim children in New Jersey who refused to recite the Pledge. The case, *Holden v. Elizabeth Board of Education*, considered whether Black Muslim children who remained silent during the Pledge could be expelled from school based on religious freedom claims. The school district claimed that the students were motivated by racial concerns, not primarily religious or political objections to the Pledge. The Court ordered the students reinstated.[12]

Attacks on the Pledge Increase in the 1970s

The numbers of challenges against the Pledge accelerated in the 1970s. In a Florida decision, *Banks v. Board of Public Instruction of Dade County* (1970–1971), the Fifth District Federal Court struck down a requirement that students who objected to the Pledge stand while the Pledge was being recited by other students. Maryland's Supreme Court struck down a similar law in 1971 in *State v. Lundquist*.[13]

Adding "under God" to the Pledge

In February 1954, the House and Senate began discussing the addition of "under God" to the Pledge of Allegiance. On February 8, the Senate opened its session with a prayer by Monsignor Bela Varga, president of the Hungarian National Council. Varga's prayer is significant because it reflects the concerns of most Americans during this period of history about international Communism:

> O Lord Almighty Father, protector of the weak and ruler of the strong. Thy humble servants lift their prayer to Thee.
>
> In our prayer we join the imploring millions whose silent invocations rise to Thee from the dark dungeons of the Iron Curtain, from the most obscure corners of the slave camps, and from the horror chambers of the secret police. Hear these prayers, O Lord, and deliver them from evil.

O Lord give us strength as Thou has given strength to Thy servant Cardinal Mindszenty. He defied the tyrant's wrath until condemned to prison five years ago today. On this anniversary help us to dedicate ourselves with renewed firmness and a sure hope to work for Thy peace on earth and for Thy love among men.

On this anniversary, standing in this mighty bastion of freedom's strength, we invoke Thy providence, O Ruler of Nations, that we may justify the confidence of millions of Thy children, who are now bent but unbroken under the scourge of despotism and in the darkness of slavery. Have mercy on them and let us be led by Thy mighty hand that we may strengthen their unquenching hope to see the end of all tyranny.

We entreat Thee, O Father in Heaven. Lend Thy wisdom in all our deliberations and extend the light of Thy grace when we ponder the fate of centuries to come. Bestow upon us the endowments of Thy divine benevolence that this Chamber, that this Capitol remain the fortress of man's God-given right to life, liberty, and the pursuit of happiness, a beacon to dispel the dark forces of death, tyranny, and the very denial of Thy Holy Name.

Almighty Creator who hast made all men in Thine image and likeness free, give us strength to drive out the abominations of tyranny which defile Thy kingdom on earth. God bless you all. Amen.[14]

On February 18, 1954, Representative Oliver P. Bolton (R-OH) rose to express support for adding "under God" to the Pledge. His inspiring words are worth reprinting:

Mr. Speaker, I rise today to add my voice to that of several of my esteemed colleagues who have proposed that the words "under God" be added to the Pledge of Allegiance to the flag of the United States.

Since having the privilege of attending the annual dinner of the Washington Pilgrimage of American Churchmen in 1953, at which this proposal was made, I have been studying it and discussing it with constituents in my district of various religious denominations.

I am able to report that the suggestion appears to have the support of Protestants, Catholics, and Jews alike, and I believe that there is strong public sentiment in favor of adding a recognition of the Deity to this pledge which is recited daily in schools across the Nation and on many patriotic occasions.

Particularly does it seem appropriate to offer this resolution in the period when we are commemorating the birthdays of two great Presidents, Lincoln and Washington, who repeatedly expressed the conviction that our Nation needs to recognize God if it is to maintain true greatness.

It was Abraham Lincoln who first used the expression, "this Nation under God," in his immortal Gettysburg Address.

History records no stronger exhortation to the American people to recognize the sovereignty of God than that which Lincoln voiced in his proclamation of March 30, 1863, calling for a national day of prayer. Speaking—as he might have done to Americans of this day, too—Lincoln said: "We have been the recipients of the choicest bounty of heaven; we have grown in numbers, wealth, and power as no other nation has ever grown. But we have forgotten God. We have forgotten the gracious hand which preserved us in peace and enriched and strengthened us, and we have vainly imagined in the deceitfulness of our hearts, that all these blessings were produced by some superior wisdom and virtue of our own. Intoxicated with unbroken success, we have become too self-sufficient to feel the necessity of redeeming and preserving grace, too proud to the God that made us."

I am reminded, too, Mr. Speaker, as I offer this resolution, of the words of George Washington in his first inaugural at New York City April 30, 1789, when he said: "No people can be bound to acknowledge and adore the invisible hand which conducts the affairs of men more than those of the United States. Every step by which we have advanced to the character of an independent nation seems to have been distinguished by some token of providential agency."

President Washington acknowledged that sovereignty of God in the affairs of men which Samuel Adams so aptly expressed when, upon signing of the Declaration of Independence severing the Colonies from the rule of George III, he remarked: "We have this day restored the sovereign, to whom men alone ought to be obedient. He reigns in heaven."

Our own great President of this day, Dwight D. Eisenhower, has repeatedly in his public utterances expressed the conviction that except as America recognizes the spiritual foundation of our democratic institutions and the divine God-given dignity of man, we cannot preserve these free institutions against the forces of atheistic materialism which surround us.

It is my belief that if we daily pledge allegiance to our flag as a symbol of "one nation under God, indivisible, with liberty and justice for all," we shall be reaffirming a basic truth. Our pledge of allegiance is not complete without a recognition of our basic faith.

Mr. Speaker, I am happy to join with my colleagues, Mr. Rabaut, Mr. Pillion, Mr. Miller of New York, and Mr. Oakman, in giving bipartisan, interfaith support to this proposal. It is my sincere hope that we will listen to the words of Lincoln, Washington, and other great men and will add this recognition of basic faith to our affirmation of our loyalty.[15]

In debates, the Senate was nearly unanimous in its support of adding "under God" to the Pledge. The only senator who expressed any doubt about it was Senator Kenneth Keating of New York, who expressed concern that changing the wording might compromise the Pledge as a "work of American literature." In Keating's statement, published in the *Congressional Record* for June 7, 1954, he noted:

> . . . I believe it is appropriate to call attention to the impropriety of projecting the Congress of the United States too far into this field of rewriting American literature. The Pledge of Allegiance is a priceless gem of American prose, comparable in many respects to Lincoln's Gettysburg Address. True, the Congress has already seen fit to assume jurisdiction over the pledge by previous changes in wording, and now is about to make another change. I think in the future we should tread very lightly in this field. A warning was sounded to me, very properly, by the devoted son of the distinguished author of the Pledge of Allegiance, Francis Bellamy, whom I have the honor to number among my constituents and personal friends. He is David Bellamy, of 64 Barrington Street, Rochester, New York. His literary father is a graduate of the University of Rochester in the class of 1876.
>
> Mr. Bellamy points out quite correctly, that the Pledge earned its place in literature and in the hearts of people because of its completeness, simplicity, and perfection of style, and that its value is in the simple manner in which it has expressed its singleness of purpose. He asks what other classic in American literature has been altered by Congress, to which I have been forced to reply that I know of none.
>
> Therefore, while I feel sure the change now suggested will and should receive unanimous favor in this Congress, I do think we should move with extreme caution in this field."[16]

After the resolution was passed and signed into law by President Eisenhower a few critics began to emerge—but not from Congress. The Episcopal journal *Living Church* editorialized against the adding of "under God." The editorialist wrote: "The invocation of the Almighty . . . is serious business. God is not easily flattered. . . . So let us not understand 'under God' as a declaration of national righteousness." Political commentator William Lee Miller said the addition of "under God" was a vague, watered-down spirituality that stood for nothing. He observed: "The popular religious revival is closely tied to a popular patriotism, of which it is the uncritical ally. Religion and Americanism, God and country, Cross and flag. The two pieties combine in much public discourse, and often the American will slide unnoticing from one to another."[17]

There was actually very little criticism of the addition of "under God" to the Pledge of Allegiance, primarily because Americans were still devout in their religious beliefs and they were patriotic. They knew they were facing a godless enemy in international Communism. Moreover, they had just seen the end of the Korean War, in which thousands of American boys had died on the battlefield fighting the North Koreans and the Red Chinese.

"Under God" was added to the Pledge to make a clear statement of our nation's religious roots and to make a clear distinction between our nation and the atheistic Communist dictatorships that were springing up around the world.

Catholic Representative Louis Rabaut (D-MI) was one of the leaders of the effort to add "under God" to the Pledge. Congressman Rabaut explained his reasoning by saying: "It is my hope that the recitation of the Pledge, with this addition of 'under God,' by our school children will bring to them a deeper understanding of the real meaning of patriotism." In 1953, Congressman Rabaut sponsored another related bill that would have created a postal cancellation mark stating: "In God We Trust."

He recommended the cancellation mark because, he said, "It is an especially appropriate time to re-proclaim our adherence to this historic motto. It strikes at the philosophical roots of communism, atheism, and materialism."

After Rabaut learned about Reverend George Docherty's powerful sermon on the Pledge in front of President Eisenhower, he observed: "Dr. Docherty and I are not of the same Christian denomination, but I say that he has hit the nail right on the head. You may argue from dawn till dusk about differing political, economic, and social systems, but the fundamental issue which is the unbridgeable gap between America and Communist Russia is a belief in the Almighty God. From the root of atheism stems the evil weed of communism. Unless we are willing to affirm our belief in the existence of God, we open the floodgates to tyranny and oppression."[18] Earlier, as he was lobbying for the addition of "under God" to the Pledge, Rep. Rabaut described in detail his thoughts on the Pledge and "under God":

> It is, therefore, most proper that in our salute to the flag, the patriotic standard around which we rally as Americans, we state the real meaning of the flag. From their earliest childhood our children must know the real meaning of America. Children and Americans of all ages must know that this is one Nation in which "under God" means "liberty and justice for all" (*Congressional Record*, February 12, 1954).

The Pledge Is a Statement of Loyalty to God and Country

For more than 114 years, the Pledge of Allegiance has been recited by millions of children in our public schools as a statement of loyalty to our nation and system of government. Since 1954, millions of children have recited "under God" as part of the Pledge. Atheist Michael Newdow's efforts to remove "under

God" from the Pledge will ultimately fail if—and only if—Americans rein in the federal courts and restrict their authority to rule on such important issues as religious freedom. This is why Congress must pass the Pledge Protection Act. *The federal courts, including the Supreme Court, have shown they are incapable of issuing constitutionally correct rulings on this vital freedom.* As we have seen, religious freedom in America is actually the "first freedom," and it was this desire for religious freedom that led to the founding of this great nation.

As we will discuss in Chapter 8, Congress has constitutional authority to create, abolish, or limit the appellate jurisdiction of federal courts. Liberals will claim that tampering with federal courts is threatening "judicial independence," but the Constitution grants no such independence to federal judges. To do so would create what Judge Robert Bork has correctly called a "judicial oligarchy."

Thomas Jefferson wisely warned against the belief that judges are free from any constraints on their rulings. In 1820, Jefferson wrote a letter to William C. Jarvis about judicial despotism. His prophetic warning is now a reality in our nation:

> To consider the judges as the ultimate arbiters of all constitutional questions [is] a very dangerous doctrine indeed, and one which would place us under the despotism of an oligarchy. Our judges are as honest as other men and not more so. They have with others the same passions for party, for power, and the privilege of their corps. Their maxim is *boni judicus est amplaire jurisdictionem* [good justice is broad jurisdiction], and their power the more dangerous as they are in office for life and not responsible, as the other functionaries are, to the elective control. The Constitution has erected no such single tribunal, knowing that to whatever hands confided, with the corruptions of time and party, its members would become despots. It

has more wisely made all the departments co-equal and co-sovereign within themselves.[19]

In a letter to Edward Livingston in 1819, Jefferson expressed the same sentiment about the dangers of an out-of-control judiciary:

> This member of the Government [Judiciary] was at first considered as the most harmless and helpless of all its organs. But it has proved that the power of declaring what the law is, *ad libitum*, [at will] by sapping and mining slyly and without alarm the foundations of the Constitution, can do what open force would not dare to attempt.[20]

In essence, Jefferson considered the federal court system to be a subversive influence in our republic because it continually undermined constitutional government by usurping power rightly belonging to the executive and legislative branches of government.

Jefferson was correct to worry about the unrestrained power of the judiciary to reinterpret the Constitution and, by doing so, to undermine it. Many federal judges view themselves as above the White House and the Congress in their power to impose their political agendas on Americans. The far-left judges on the Ninth Circuit Court in San Francisco are the worst offenders in this regard. Three judges on this court ruled that "under God" was unconstitutional—thanks to the efforts of atheist Michael Newdow. In Chapter 7, we will discuss Newdow's case, the radical Ninth Circuit Court, and other outrageous federal court decisions that have, in Jefferson's words, "sapp[ed] and min[ed] slyly and without alarm the foundations of the Constitution."

The Pledge Protection Act will restrict the unrestrained power of far-left judges to undermine the Constitution and is specifically aimed at restricting federal courts from ruling on issues involving the Pledge of Allegiance.

CHAPTER 5

"Under God" in the Pledge

A S I noted in chapter 3, the battle to add "under God" to the Pledge came out of a national concern about international Communism and its atheistic philosophy, which glorified the all-powerful state at the expense of individual freedom.

Winston Churchill's famous "Iron Curtain" speech in 1946 was an alarming message to Americans about the dangers posed by Soviet Communist plans for worldwide domination. Churchill wisely warned:

> We cannot be blind to the fact that the liberties enjoyed by individual citizens throughout the United States and throughout the British Empire are not valid in a considerable number of countries, some of which are very powerful. In these States control is enforced upon the common people by various kinds of all-embracing police governments to a degree which is overwhelming and contrary to every principle of democracy. The power of the State is exercised without restraint, either by dictators or by compact oligarchies operating through a privileged party and a political police.[1]

In 1948, the House Committee on Un-American Activities began holding hearings on the Communist influences in

Hollywood, and that same year, former Communist Whittaker Chambers went public with accusations that he had been in a secret Communist cell with Alger Hiss in the 1930s. Hiss was a darling of the liberal left at the time, having served as assistant secretary of state and as secretary general of the United Nations at its founding conference in 1945. After there was ample evidence Chambers was telling the truth, Hiss was convicted of perjury for lying about his involvement in a Communist cell. He spent five years in prison but went to his grave denying that he was a spy for the Soviet Union within the American government. The Venona papers (transcripts of KGB and GRU messages during World War II) were released in the mid-1990s, proving without doubt that Hiss was working for the Soviet Union—even up to 1945, when he helped establish the United Nations.

Chambers published his best-selling book *Witness* in 1952, describing his disillusionment with atheistic Communism and his return to his Catholic faith. In his book, Chambers made an important point—and one we should all consider in view of the current culture war we're fighting. *He said America was suffering from a crisis of faith and he accused liberalism of being simply a watered-down version of Communism.* In essence, he saw the battle for America as being a war between atheism/secularism versus faith in a transcendent God who gives meaning and order to our lives!

In *Witness,* Whittaker Chambers introduces his story as a Soviet spy by writing a letter to his children. In it, he tells them:

[the West] . . . fails to grasp that, for it, the only possible answer to the Communist challenge: Faith in God or Faith in Man? is the challenge: Faith in God. Economics is not the central problem of this century. It is a relative problem which can be solved in relative ways. Faith is the central problem of this age. The Western world does not know it, but it already possesses the answer to this problem—but only provided that its faith in God and the freedom He enjoins is as great as Communism's faith in Man.[2]

Whittaker Chambers tried to warn America of the dangers of losing faith in God and turning instead to secularism and liberalism. His book awakened millions of Americans to these truths. Included in that group was a young man named Ronald Reagan, who often quoted Chambers as he developed his own political ideas about the future of our nation and the threat of Soviet domination of the world. Reagan's final philosophy was boiled down into four words: "We win, they lose." During his eight years as president, he brought down the Soviet Union by the force of his will and his unwavering faith in God and in the moral strength of this nation under God!

Communist Expansionism

In 1949, a year after Chambers shocked the nation with his accusation against Alger Hiss, Americans saw the ominous reach of Communism into China, when that nation fell to Mao Tse-tung's vicious dictatorship and the anti-Communist Chinese fled to Taiwan to escape enslavement under Mao's totalitarian state.

More Communist expansionism occurred in 1950 when the North Koreans invaded South Korea and American soldiers were drawn into a bloody no-win war until a truce was agreed to in 1953.

It was also in 1953 that the hit TV series *I Led Three Lives* began airing nationally. This three-year series dramatized the story of Herbert Philbrick, who had worked undercover in a Communist cell for the FBI during the 1940s. Philbrick's secret life came to light in 1949 when he testified before a government committee in New York against members of the Communist Party USA.

All these political and cultural milestones in our nation's history made Americans very much aware of the dangers of international Communism and its atheistic ideas. To counter this atheistic belief system, citizen's groups and their allies in Congress wanted to make a clear public statement about our nation's founding upon God's laws. One way to do this was to add "under God" to the Pledge.

It was—and still is—a tenet of Communism that religion is an enemy of mankind and must be suppressed. Communist tyrants believe the state is all-powerful and has the right to kill and conquer in the name of Communism. Religious people are considered disloyal because they refuse to worship the state as god. The first-century Christians had the same conflict with the Caesars of Rome; they refused to worship Caesar as god and were thrown to the lions for their refusal to worship the state.

A Short History of Atheistic Communism

In a discussion of the Pledge of Allegiance and "under God," as well as the effort to get "In God We Trust" on our coins and as our national motto, it is important to understand the atheistic roots of Communism.

In his classic work *The Naked Communist,* former FBI agent W. Cleon Skousen provided a horrifying history of Communism from its beginnings in the mind of Karl Marx to the seizure of Cuba in 1959 by dictator Fidel Castro.

Marx, of course, was an atheist who hated those who had faith in God and all religions. In fact, he chose as his personal motto that of the Greek mythological character Prometheus, who cried out: "In one word—I hate all the gods!" Marx was driven by a hatred of Christianity and believed that human consciousness was the highest divinity that existed. As a result of this hatred, Marx developed a philosophy that has resulted in the deaths of millions of people throughout the world and the ongoing torture of Christians for their faith in God.

Marx's hate-filled philosophy against capitalism and religion inspired Lenin as he and the Bolsheviks overthrew the czar of Russia in 1917 and helped spread totalitarian atheism throughout the world during the twentieth century.

It was Lenin who implemented Karl Marx's murderous ideas, and Lenin's hatred of Christians and all religion was a basic tenet of his Marxist philosophy. Lenin clearly stated it in his position statement on religion: "We must combat religion—this is the ABC of all materialism, and consequently Marxism."[3]

In an official statement in the *Young Bolshevik*, published in 1946, the Soviet Communist Party states: "The philosophy of Marxism-Leninism—the theoretical foundation of the Communist Party—is incompatible with religion." Lenin also said, "A young man or woman cannot be a Communist youth unless he or she is free of religious convictions."

What is the official atheistic Communist view of the Bible? A Soviet Russian dictionary published in 1951 described the Bible as "a collection of fantastic legends without any scientific support. It is full of dark hints, historical mistakes and contradictions. It serves as a factor for gaining power and subjugating the unknowing nations."[4]

In *The Naked Communist*, Skousen described what he called the "Homo-Marxian" man—a man who rejected morality and had no conscience. He was willing to do whatever was needed to conquer and enslave people under Communism. If they resisted, he would kill them without regret. Skousen noted: "Marxist Man has convinced himself that nothing is evil which answers the call to expediency. He has released himself from all the confining restraints of honor and ethics which mankind has previously tried to use as a basis for harmonious human relations."[5]

And what has the world suffered at the hands of the atheist Homo-Marxian Man during the past 80 years of human history?

The answer is slavery, death, torture, misery, poverty, famine, and endless pain.

Former University of Hawaii political science professor R. J. Rummel has studied the incredibly violent nature of governments who murder their own people. In 1994, Rummel published detailed research on the massive slaughters of human beings that took place in the twentieth century and earlier. In *Death by Government*, Rummel lists the nations that have killed millions of their own people in what he calls "democide."

Rummel observes that "peace" under totalitarian regimes is actually more lethal than war. He says,

> Putting the human cost of war and democide together, Power [meaning tyrannical rule] has killed over 203 million people in this century. . . . Even if all to be said about absolute Power was that it causes war and the attendant slaughter of the young and most capable . . . this would be enough, But worse even without the excuse of combat, Power also massacres in cold blood those helpless people it controls—in fact, *several times more of them*.[6]

What nations have routinely killed millions of their own people over the past century? The list is a combination of militant atheistic Communist, Fascist, or ruthless Muslim regimes: Soviet Russia, Communist China, Khmer Rouge-dominated Cambodia, Vietnam, Yugoslavia under Tito, Nazi Germany, and Turkey.

Rummel points out on his Web site that Soviet Russia under Lenin, Stalin, and subsequent dictators murdered more than 61 million Russians in order to terrorize the nation and keep the people enslaved. In *Death by Government*, he writes: "In total, during the first eighty-eight years of this century, almost 170 million men, women, and children have been shot, beaten, tortured, knifed, burned, starved, frozen, crushed, or worked to death; buried alive, drowned, hung, bombed, or killed in any other of the myriad ways governments have inflicted deaths on unarmed, helpless citizens and foreigners. The dead could conceivably be nearly 360 million people."[7]

Professor Rummel notes that the Communist revolution in Russia in 1917 ushered in the era of totalitarian governments. However, it was more than a revolution. Rummel says it "was not just a seizure of power and change of leadership but a revolutionary transformation in the very nature and worldview of governance. It was the creation of a unique reason-of-state and the institution of an utterly cold-blooded social engineering view of the state's power over its people." Rummel quotes Lenin, who clearly stated his theoretical foundation for creating an atheistic terror state: "The scientific concept of dictatorship means nothing else but this—Power without limit, resting directly upon force, restrained by no laws, absolutely unrestrained by rules."[8]

The many millions of individuals slaughtered by their own governments during the twentieth century were primarily killed by atheists, Fascists, and ruthless pro-German Muslims in Turkey between 1915 and 1923. The Turks forced millions of Christian Armenians on death marches into the desert. They died along the way, were thrown off cliffs, burned alive, or drowned in rivers. The Turks began this slaughter of Armenians because they feared they would side with Russia against the Germans in World War I. An estimated 1.5 million Armenian Christians were killed by the Turks during this democide.

During the twentieth century, atheists and Muslims, not Christians, were responsible for the slaughter of more than 306 million men, women, and children living under various totalitarian systems. Officially atheistic governments during the twentieth century murdered more of their own citizens than those who died in all the wars in all the recorded history of mankind. On the other hand, it was Christian nations like the United States and Britain that led the war effort in World Wars I and II, the Korean War, and the Vietnam War to protect the God-given human rights of those who were being enslaved by Communist and Fascist governments. America, for example, went to war in Korea to defend South Koreans from atheistic Communist expansionism, and lost more than 57,000 soldiers in South Vietnam to defend that nation from slaughter.

To prove America's dedication to religious freedom the Clinton administration sent U.S. armed forces to war in the Balkans to protect Muslim interests against those of our traditional Christian Serbian allies. Under President George W. Bush, America went to war in Afghanistan to defeat the brutal Islamic Taliban regime and then to Iraq, ostensibly to free that nation from the Baathist Party, which was modeled directly after the Nazi Party of Germany. Unfortunately, the Christian idea of religious liberty is a concept mostly lost on the Islamic faithful. Within a short time after we freed Afghanistan from Taliban oppression, the democratically elected Muslim government was sentencing converts from Islam to Christianity to death. The concept of religious freedom with religious tolerance, as envisioned by the founders of our nation, was developed from a Christian perspective.

In God We Trust

Liberal journalists and historians still snidely refer to the 1950s as the era of the "Red Scare," and ridicule the so-called "anti-Communist hysteria." Liberals, now just as then, are not swayed by the facts about the reality of the infiltration of our government by Communist subversives or about the march of Communism in nation after nation. Conservatives of that era were ridiculed as "red baiters" and lunatics, but they were correct about Communism. Liberals, as usual, were wrong.

It was anti-Communist and religious Americans who understood the dangers of Communism to our way of life—and who set about to make strong symbolic statements designed to teach young people to value our moral system, based upon God's laws.

Patriotic congressmen and grassroots organizations like the American Legion, Daughters of the American Revolution, and Knights of Columbus all took leading roles in promoting "under God" in our Pledge. This was considered an important symbolic gesture and an educational tool to teach children the value of our religious heritage. During this same time period, an effort was under way to make certain "In God We Trust" became our national motto and was printed on our coins and currency.

The history of "In God We Trust" parallels the efforts to add "under God" to the Pledge—and even predates the Pledge by thirty years—back to the Civil War.

In fact, religious statements about God were printed on American coins as far back as 1694, when the colony of Carolina printed "God preserve Carolina and the Lord's Proprietors" on a one-cent piece. A New England token printed that same year bore the inscription "God preserve New England."[9]

Louisiana minted a coin in 1721 that carried the words "Blessed be the name of the Lord." In 1849, Utah minted a coin that said "Holiness of the Lord" on it.

The words "In God We Trust" first appeared on American coins in 1864 through the efforts of the Reverend M. R. Watkinson of Ridleyville, Pennsylvania. On November 13, 1861, Watkinson wrote a letter of concern to Secretary of the Treasury Samuel P. Chase. In his letter, he said: "One fact touching our currency has hitherto been seriously overlooked. I mean the recognition of the Almighty God in some form in our coins." He told Chase that putting an inscription like "God, liberty, and Law" on our currency "would place us openly under the divine protection we have personally claimed." He considered a "national shame in disowning God as not the least of our present national disasters."[10]

Secretary Chase agreed with Reverend Watkinson and sent a letter to James Pollock, director of the U.S. Mint. Chase told

Pollock: "No nation can be strong except in the strength of God, or safe except in His defense. The trust of our people in God should be declared on our national coins." He directed Pollock to create a design with a motto expressing "in the fewest and tersest words possible this national recognition."[11]

In 1862, the Mint had designed a half dollar and half eagle that had the inscription "God our Trust" on it. In 1863, a two-cent piece had "God and our Country" engraved on it. In December 1863, Pollock submitted designs for one-, two-, and three-cent pieces with "Our country; our God" and "God our trust" on them. Chase approved the designs but suggested that the motto be changed to "In God We Trust."[12]

Congress had to authorize the addition of the motto on coins. In March 1865, Congress approved the minting of a three-cent piece with "In God We Trust" on it. The bill sailed through the House and Senate without debate and without any amendments added to it. Later, the motto was added to other coins and remained on these coins until the early 1900s.

Theodore Roosevelt Removes Motto

After Theodore Roosevelt was elected to the presidency in 1904, he spoke with Treasury Secretary Leslie M. Shaw about what he called the "artistically atrocious hideousness" of American coins.

President Roosevelt was determined to create a whole new set of coins without "In God We Trust" on them. He commissioned artist Augustus Saint-Gaudens to design a coin that reflected the artistry on ancient Greek coins. Saint-Gaudens was eager to design a new set of coins, but told Roosevelt that the inclusion of "In God We Trust" was an "inartistic intrusion" and suggested it be deleted. Roosevelt authorized the deletion, but he ran into strong opposition not only from the Treasury Department, but also from members of Congress.[13]

In his battle to get new coins minted along the lines of Greek coinage, he wrote to Saint-Gaudens: "I think it [the redesign] will seriously increase the mortality among the employees of the mint at seeing such a desecration, but they will perish in a good cause."

Roosevelt continued to fight for the redesign and came to believe that the "In God We Trust" motto represented "irreverence which comes dangerously close to sacrilege." He thought the inscription cheapened the sentiment "just as it would be to cheapen it by use on postage stamps, or in advertisements."[14] Protests against removing the "In God We Trust" motto from American coins not only came from Congressional leaders but from newspaper editorial pages. The *Atlanta Constitution* claimed Americans would have to choose between Roosevelt and God. A poem published by an outraged citizen in the *New York Sun* said:

In God We Trust
Upon Our Coins!
Oh, sacrilegious people!
God is not needed in this nation;
We have the great Administration;
And he's enough for all creation
Our Teddy.[15]

Congressmen attacked the new Greek-inspired coin designs on the floor of the House. Rep. Morris Sheppard (D-TX) led the attack against the new design with a passionate floor address on January 7, 1908. He described the importance of religion in American life and then attacked the newly designed coin, "which shows on one side a woman in savage headdress, on the other a Roman eagle in predatory flight—the one side a degradation of woman, the other a eulogy of war?"[16]

The Committee on Coinage, Weights, and Measures debated the new coin designs and the removal of the motto acknowledging God in American life. The committee unanimously approved passage of a bill to reverse the President's attempt to redesign the coins and remove "In God We Trust" from them. The Committee stated that "as a Christian nation" the motto should be restored as "evidence to all the nations of the world that the best and only reliance for the perpetuation of the republican institution is upon a Christian patriotism, which, recognizing the universal fatherhood of God, appeals to the universal brotherhood of man as the source of the authority and power of all just government."[17]

In debates on the House floor over Roosevelt's effort to remove the motto from our coins, Rep. Charles C. Carlin applauded the coinage committee's actions and said it provided a "lesson to the country and the world to the effect that this is a Christian nation, and that this body is composed of patriotic Americans who, regardless of party affiliations, fearlessly discharge a public duty when they are once convinced there is a duty to be discharged."

Rep. Ollie M. James was just as passionate as Carlin in expressing support for the motto. He said Roosevelt was making a great mistake and affirmed that the United States is "not only a Christian nation, but we are engaged in sending to foreign countries and to distant people our missionaries to preach the religions of Jesus Christ, and we want our money so that when this gold that you say is so good goes across the ocean and is held in the hands of those who do not know of the existence of the Saviour of the world, we can say: 'Here are the dollars of the greatest nation on earth; one that does not put its trust in floating navies or in marching armies, but places its trust in God.' "[18]

Rep. James said that "In God We Trust" reflected the beliefs of the founders of our nation, and the fact that belief in a Supreme Being "is breathed in the Declaration of Independence, lives in the Constitution, hallows the oath we take at the bar of this House. It inspired our soldiers to fight at Bunker Hill, to suffer at Valley Forge, to triumph at Yorktown."[19]

Rep. Charles G. Edwards of Georgia was also adamant about preserving the motto: "The Methodist, the Baptist, the Presbyterian, the Catholic, the Hebrews, the Episcopal, in fact all churches, all creeds, who have a belief in God, are as one in the opinion that it was a great mistake to ever have removed this motto from our coins, and they are one in the sentiment that this motto shall be restored." He also felt that all public offices should be held by God-fearing men: "A man who is not sound in his belief in God has no right in high office, which is the gift of a God-fearing people."[20]

One of the few legislators to protest the motto was Gustav Kustermann (R-WI). He objected to the motto "because I do not believe in any religion that in order to thrive needs advertising, nor do I believe in any person that always hangs out his shingle, 'I am a Christian.' "[21]

Legislation mandating the "In God We Trust" inscription on certain coins became law in May 1908 with an overwhelming vote of 259 for, 5 against, and 4 answering "present." The inscription thus became mandatory on a few selected American coins.

In 1955, during the height of America's concern over Communist expansionism throughout the world, Congress passed legislation requiring "In God We Trust" to be placed on our paper currency. The legislation also required—for the first time—that the inscription be added to all American coins, not just a selected few.

During the floor debate over this legislation, Charles Bennett (D-FL) argued that "nothing can be more certain than that our country was founded in a spiritual atmosphere and with a firm trust in God." Bennett warned, "These days when imperialistic and materialistic Communism seeks to attack and destroy freedom, we should continuously look for ways to strengthen the foundations of our freedom. At the base of our freedom is our faith in God and the desire of Americans to live by His will and by His guidance. As long as this country trusts in God, it will prevail."[22]

There was such unanimity of purpose in both the House and Senate over this legislation that no one spoke in opposition in either chamber! In fact, in 1956, Congress passed legislation making "In God We Trust" our national motto—not only an inscription on our coins and paper currency.

In supporting the passage of legislation making "In God We Trust" our national motto, the Senate Committee on the Judiciary pointed to the fact that "The Star-Spangled Banner" (our national anthem) contained the words, "And this be our motto— 'In God is our trust.'" The committee believed that our nation needed "In God We Trust" as the national motto because it would "be of great spiritual and psychological value to our country to have a clearly designated national motto of inspirational quality in plain, popular accepted English."[23]

Even before Congress enacted legislation making "In God We Trust" our national motto, this inscription had been placed on the walls of the Senate and House. In the Senate, mottos acknowledging God were carved in marble over three entrances. Those mottos are: *Annuit Coeptis* ("God has favored our undertakings"); *Novus Ordo Seclorum* ("A new order of the ages is born"); and In God We Trust.

In 1962, the House of Representatives added "In God We Trust" above the chair of the Speaker of the House. This decision came just a few months after the Supreme Court, in *Engle v. Vitale,* struck down a New York law requiring students to say a prayer each morning before the beginning of classes. Rep. William J. Randall (D-MO) said the reason for adding the motto above the Speaker's chair was "that we have given perhaps not directly but yet in a not so subtle way our answer to the recent decision of the U.S. Supreme Court banning the regent's prayer from the New York State schools."[24] Clearly, even as far back as 1962, Congress was far more favorable to religious expression than was the left-leaning Supreme Court. Members of Congress apparently still had a consciousness of our religious heritage and the fact our entire system of government was based upon a belief that God gives us rights. We do not receive them from the government.

American Atheists Attack "In God We Trust"

My mother, Madalyn Murray O'Hair, crusaded for (among other things) removing "In God We Trust" from our coins and paper currency. In 1978, her American Atheists group filed a lawsuit against W. Michael Blumenthal, secretary of the Treasury, to have "In God We Trust" declared to be an unconstitutional endorsement of religion by the federal government. The case, *Madalyn Murray O'Hair v. W. Michael Blumenthal, Secretary of the Treasury,* was rejected by the Fifth Circuit Court of Appeals in Texas that year. It noted that the use of "In God We Trust" "is of a patriotic or ceremonial character and bears no true resemblance to a governmental sponsorship of religious exercise." Even the radically liberal Ninth Circuit Court of Appeals in San Francisco found this to be too extreme for them. The Ninth Circuit, in the 1970 case of *Aronow v. United States,* reached the same conclusion as the Fifth Circuit.[25]

President Eisenhower Supported Religious Expression

The mid-1950s was a significant time in America's spiritual history. Congress not only added "under God" to the Pledge of Allegiance and made "In God We Trust" our national motto, but President Eisenhower lent his support to an American Legion "Back to God" program in 1955. This program was designed to encourage Americans to reconfirm their reliance on

God and to promote patriotism in the face of a ruthless atheistic Communist enemy. President Eisenhower told the American Legion: "Without God, there could be no American form of Government, nor an American way of life. Recognition of the Supreme Being is the first—and most basic—expression of Americanism. Thus the Founding Fathers saw it, and thus, with God's help, it will continue to be."[26]

As part of the "Back to God" program, Eisenhower described the founders' belief in God and the dignity of the individual. According to Eisenhower, after the framers of the Constitution recognized God as the author of human rights, they "declared that the purpose of Government is to secure those rights." In totalitarian nations, said Eisenhower, "the State claims to be the author of human rights." If the state can give rights, "it can—and inevitably will—take away those rights."

Eisenhower clearly understood that because the Founding Fathers believed in God as the author and giver of human life and human rights, no government had the right to take those away. Our government was created to protect the rights we already possessed as creations of Almighty God.

The "Back to God" effort and the effort of Congress to put "under God" in the Pledge and make "In God We Trust" our national motto were all efforts aimed at teaching Americans that our nation was founded upon a belief in God—and that our belief in God was a bulwark against atheistic Communism.[27]

Americans in the 1950s were nearly unanimous in their belief that our nation faced a dangerous enemy—one that routinely enslaved individuals and persecuted anyone who believed in God. The essence of Communism is atheism and a belief in the state as god. Under Communism, Socialism, or Fascism, the individual has no rights. All power comes from the state and the individual is considered the property of the state. He only has whatever "rights" the state grants him.

Under these totalitarian states, the government determines what is moral or immoral; what is right or wrong. And, it severely punishes anyone who disobeys the dictatorial rule of the state.

Religious Cleansing Under Way

Our belief in religious and political freedom extends to all human beings. We still believe that human rights come from God, not governments, and that tyrannical governments deserve to be destroyed.

Unfortunately, there are evil forces at work in our own culture attempting every day to undermine the foundation of our society and our Constitution. Those atheistic forces, led by the American Civil Liberties Union and individuals like Michael Newdow, are engaging in a religious cleansing of our society—seeking to replace faith in God with an atheistic, secularist, and heartless philosophy that has no respect for the dignity of man as a creation of God.

By attempting to wipe out all vestiges of Christianity in our culture, secularists are subverting the underlying belief system upon which our laws are based, laws which protect our freedoms of speech, religion, and association. Once this religious foundation is removed, our institutions and laws will not be based upon God's moral laws or the Bill of Rights, but upon the unrestrained power of tyrants on the Supreme Court, in Congress, and in the executive branch.

If Michael Newdow and the ACLU win this war to cleanse America of its religious roots, we will end up with a ruthless system of government that will be no different in form from that of the former Soviet Union or the current atheistic regime in Communist China. Under a Newdow/ACLU America, "human rights" and morality will be determined by the unrestrained power of whoever holds office. These individuals and groups are working for a system of Lenin-like government—unrestrained by any laws.

We could face the same grim fate the Russians experienced after the Bolshevik Revolution in 1917, or that the suffering people in the Sudan currently face from their own corrupt government.

Gouverneur Morris, a signer of the U.S. Constitution, was correct when he observed: "There must be religion. When that ligament is torn, society is disjointed and its members perish. The nation is exposed to foreign violence and domestic convulsion."[28]

We should remember our history and defend our religious symbols and the Christian roots of our constitutional republic. If we permit the secularists to win, our nation will inevitably be plunged into moral chaos.

Defending "under God" in the Pledge of Allegiance and protecting "In God We Trust" on our money are two battles in the ongoing culture war. They are skirmishes in a larger war against Christianity being waged by the ACLU, People for the American Way, NOW, Americans United for Separation of Church and State, billionaire atheist/Socialist George Soros, Michael Newdow, and others. We cannot—must not—give them an inch in this battle. The battle over the Pledge must be won. We must send a strong message to the secularists and to the liberal activist judges on our federal courts that they cannot tamper with America's Christian foundations.

If the secularists succeed in removing "under God" from the Pledge, it will set a dangerous precedent and embolden them to increase their efforts to cleanse America of all traces of our Christian heritage. This is why it is so important to pass the Pledge Protection Act to block this aggressive movement. It isn't just the words "under God" that are at stake. It is the whole foundation upon which our nation was built. It is religious liberty and freedom of speech.

What is also at risk is the whole concept of morality based upon the Bible. John Quincy Adams, the sixth president of the United States, stated this case well in a letter he wrote to his son, published in 1850 in *Letters of John Quincy Adams, to His Son, on the Bible and its Teachings*. He told him:

> There are three points of doctrine the belief of which forms the foundation of all morality. The first is the existence of God; the second is the immortality of the human soul; and the third is a future state of rewards and punishments. Suppose it possible for a man to disbelieve either of these three articles of faith and that man will have no conscience, he will have no other law than that of the tiger or the shark. The laws of man may bind him in chains or may put him to death, but they never can make him wise, virtuous, or happy.[29]

If our nation is stripped of the belief in God, in the immortality of the soul, and in a future state of rewards and punishments, the American people will become as John Q. Adams stated: men without a conscience and as lawless as a tiger or a shark. Adams was describing the Homo-Marxian man and the current-day humanistic atheist, who views religious belief as the enemy of freedom. The truth of the matter is that it is the atheist who is an enemy of human freedom. As we have seen, the bloody history of the twentieth century shows that atheism is always a threat to human life and liberty. Its worldview brings death whenever it rules a society. On the other hand, Christianity typically brings freedom wherever it is practiced—especially when the principles of Christianity become the foundation of law in a nation.

CHAPTER **6**

The Modern Crusade Against the Pledge and Religious Symbols

D URING the past fifty years, there have been repeated
attacks against the Pledge of Allegiance and more
recently, specific attacks against the words "under
God." The attack typically involves a student or teacher who is
"offended" by the words "under God," or who refuses to stand
when the Pledge is recited. The mainstream media, of course,
are more than willing to turn this rebellious individual into a
defender of free speech.

As we saw in the previous chapter, the Supreme Court has
already ruled that no one can be compelled to say the Pledge.
Now, the battle line is shifting to the question of whether students and anti-Pledge teachers can sit while all of the other students stand to recite the Pledge. Michael Newdow has added a
new twist to this. In his first lawsuit against the Pledge, he
claimed his daughter was "offended" by having to listen to
"under God" recited each day in school as part of the Pledge.
(I will deal with this case in more detail in chapter 7.)

In 2005, the ever-ready-to-sue ACLU and a Maryland student challenged the faculty at Leonardtown High School in St.

Mary's County over the student's refusal to stand during the Pledge. The ACLU sent a letter of concern to the school principal outlining the "rights" students have, which apparently include the "right" not to stand during the Pledge. In addition, teachers cannot ask students to leave during the Pledge. Thankfully, teachers can still ask students to remain quiet while the Pledge is being recited, but knowing the tortured mind-set of ACLU lawyers, it probably won't be long until a lawsuit is filed claiming that students have the "constitutional" right to play rock music and yell at each other during the Pledge.[1]

Apparently, the ACLU has found a new constitutional "right"—the right not to be offended by someone else's speech. In essence, this claim to a right not to be offended gives a minority of one person (with help from an anti-Christian ACLU lawyer) the ultimate veto power over the free speech rights of everyone else in the classroom or in the nation. This is hardly what our founders imagined when they wrote the First Amendment. Free speech almost always means that someone is going to be offended by another person's speech or writings. Being offended is the price we all pay for freedom of speech and worship in our nation. Only in a George Orwell novel could the idea of silencing the free speech of the majority to avoid offending the minority be considered protecting free speech. This is apparently where legal thinking is going.

An Anti-Catholic Justice Leads the Way

The ACLU, Michael Newdow, and others claim that the words "under God" are unconstitutional because they promote religion and violate the "separation of church and state" allegedly outlined in the Constitution. (The ACLU's fingerprints have been all over such cases since the 1920s, when this anti-Christian group was founded by Communist/pacifist Roger Baldwin.)

But the U.S. Supreme Court is ultimately responsible for this national confusion over what the Constitution truly says about freedom of religion and freedom of speech. How did we get to the point where a three-judge panel on the Ninth Circuit Court of Appeals in San Francisco can claim that "under God" in the Pledge violates the Constitution?

The answer is to be found in a little-understood decision by the Supreme Court in 1947 called *Everson v. Board of Education*. The case involved a New Jersey State law that permitted local school boards to pay for the costs of transportation to and from private schools—even Catholic schools. With legal help from the ACLU, Arch Everson, a taxpayer in Ewing Township, sued the board of education. He claimed paying for transportation to a Catholic school was indirect aid to religion and thus violated the New Jersey Constitution and the First Amendment. Everson lost his case in a lower New Jersey court, but then appealed to the Supreme Court.

The case was decided by the Supreme Court on February 10, 1947. The majority opinion was written by Associate Justice Hugo Black, but an ACLU lawyer named Leo Pheffer actually wrote a draft of the opinion that has become, just as it was intended, a tool to cleanse our nation of its religious heritage.

Justice Black's decision was actually a victory for the board of education. The decision said the state law was permissible. Black, however, used his power on the Court to insert a poison pill into the decision that has resulted in decades of anti-religious decisions from the Supreme Court and other federal judges.

The poison pill was his definition of the Establishment of Religion clause in the Constitution and his claim that the First Amendment's restrictions upon the federal government also applied to the states through the Fourteenth Amendment. Up until this decision, no court had claimed that the First Amendment applied to the sovereign states. Black claimed the

Establishment clause prohibited states from passing laws that "aid one religion, aid all religions, or prefer one religion over another."

And in his most famous sentence in the entire decision, Black claimed that Thomas Jefferson wanted a wall of separation between church and state that was high and impregnable. Black's scholarship and his motivations have come into question in recent years over this decision and its impact on religious freedom in America.

Here is Black's key statement in his ruling:

> The "establishment of religion" clause of the First Amendment means at least this: Neither a state nor the Federal Government can set up a church. Neither can pass laws which aid one religion, aid all religions, or prefer one religion over another. Neither can force nor influence a person to go to or to remain away from church against his will or force him to profess a belief or disbelief in any religion. No person can be punished for entertaining or professing religious beliefs or disbeliefs, for church attendance or non-attendance. No tax in any amount, large or small, can be levied to support any religious activities or institutions, whatever they may be called, or whatever form they may adopt to teach or practice religion. Neither a state nor the Federal Government can, openly or secretly, participate in the affairs of any religious organizations or groups and vice versa. In the words of Jefferson, the clause against establishment of religion by law was intended to erect "a wall of separation between Church and State." *Reynolds v. United States,* supra, 98 U.S. at page 164.[2]

Black also stated in his decision, "The First Amendment has erected a wall between church and state. That wall must be kept high and impregnable. We could not approve the slightest breach."[3]

Black's statement that the First Amendment was designed to forbid states from establishing state-sponsored churches is historically incorrect. In 1775, nine colonies had established churches although the number declined as the Revolution approached. Many New England states had state-endorsed Congregationalist churches and Southern states favored Episcopalian churches.

As author M. Stanton Evans pointed out in a 1995 essay in *National Review*, "At the time of the Constitutional Convention, the three New England states [Massachusetts, Connecticut, and New Hampshire] still had their Congregational establishments. In other states, there remained a network of official sanctions for religious belief, principally the requirement that one profess a certain kind of Christian doctrine to hold public office or enjoy other legal privileges."[4]

Evans also pointed out that official support for religious faith and religious requirements for public office lasted long after adoption of the First Amendment. The established church in Massachusetts, for example, wasn't abolished until 1833. In Maryland, the stipulation one had to be a Christian to hold office lasted until 1826. "As late as 1835, one had to be a Protestant to take office in North Carolina; until 1968, the requirement was that one had to be a Christian; thereafter that one had to profess a belief in God," noted Evans.[5]

In fact, as Evans points out, Thomas Jefferson himself made it clear it was the federal government that was to be prohibited from meddling in the affairs of the church or the free exercise of religion. In responding to a Presbyterian clergyman about his attitudes toward Thanksgiving proclamations, Jefferson responded:

> I consider the government of the United States as interdicted from intermeddling with religious institutions, their doctrines, discipline, or exercises. This results from the

provision that no law shall be made respecting the establishment of religion or the free exercise thereof, but also from
that which reserves to the states the powers not delegated to
the United States. Certainly no power over religious discipline had been delegated to the general government. It
must thus rest with the states as far as it can be in any
human authority.[6]

That is exactly opposite from Justice Hugo Black's claim the
First Amendment prohibits states from passing laws favoring or
disfavoring one religion over another. It was routinely done in
the thirteen colonies, and the Founding Fathers did not intend
to prohibit states from operating state churches when the First
Amendment was added to the Constitution. Religion was considered to be an absolutely essential element of good government and good citizenship. As historian James Hutson noted in
Religion and the Founding of the American Republic, "The following syllogism imprinted itself so strongly on the minds of the
Founders that it became a cliché: religion promoted virtue; virtue
promoted republicanism [good citizenship]; religion promoted,
and was indispensable for, republicanism."[7]

Hutson points out that "The Christian system of behavioral
incentives/disincentives seemed to be so essential for the main-
tenance of social order that several states—Pennsylvania (1776),
Vermont (1777), South Carolina (1778) and Tennessee (1796)—
prohibited individuals from voting or holding offices who denied
the reality of a future state of rewards and punishments [in
heaven or hell]."[8]

These historical facts provide clear evidence that our
founders had no intention of applying the First Amendment to
the states. They respected states' rights and one of those rights
included supporting an established church. The First Amendment's protection of free speech and religion was directed
against the federal government. It was to protect the states and

the people from the federal government infringing upon religious freedoms at the state level.

Black's reference to Jefferson comes from a letter Jefferson wrote to the Danbury Baptist Association in 1802. The Baptists were concerned over Jefferson's views on church-state separation and wanted a clarification from him. His response was designed to assure them the federal government would not infringe upon the religious freedoms of the Baptists or any other religious denomination.

Recent scholars have dug into Black's background and reasoning in his *Everson* decision and have expressed serious concerns about his anti-Catholic bias. Black was a former member of the Ku Klux Klan, which was not only anti-black, but anti-Catholic. Two scholars have exposed Black's anti-Catholic attitudes and called into question his legal reasoning in *Everson* on the alleged separation of church and state.

American University Professor Daniel Dreisbach in *Thomas Jefferson and the Wall of Separation of Church and State* and University of Chicago Law School Professor Philip Hamburger in *Separation of Church and State* both agree Black's anti-Catholic bias was influential in his *Everson* decision. Dreisbach, for example, shows that Black's "wall of separation" differs considerably from Thomas Jefferson's view of church-state separation. Jefferson separated the institutions of church and state. He did not want a national church. Black's "wall," however, separates religion from all involvement in civil government. Jefferson's "wall" only applied to the federal government. States were free to establish state-supported churches. Black's "wall" applied to local, state, and federal governments.

Professor Dreisbach points out that Jefferson could never have meant that the Constitution required a complete separation of religion from public life. Jefferson attended church in the House Chamber while President, and in 1802 he negotiated a treaty with the Kaskaskia Indians providing federal money to pay for the construction of a Catholic Church and the salary of a Catholic priest. Clearly, Jefferson's view of church-state separation differed considerably from Black's view.[9]

Philip Hamburger's *Separation of Church and State* was reviewed by Judge Robert Bork for the American Enterprise Institute in October 2002. In his review, Bork credits Hamburger with clearly debunking the modern myth of separation of church and state perpetuated by Black in *Everson*. Hamburger also correctly describes the nature of Hugo Black's anti-Catholic attitudes and the fact that Black was a Ku Klux Klan *leader*, not simply a member. In addition, a little-known fact is that all nine Supreme Court justices agreed with the *Everson* decision—and at least seven of these justices were members of the Masonic Lodge—a group that has historically been anti-Catholic in its attitudes.[10]

Judge Bork observes it is impossible to read Supreme Court decisions from *Everson* until the present without "recognizing what Chief Justice Rehnquist called a 'bitter hostility' toward any government recognition of religion." Bork continued:

> Hamburger does . . . rightly stress the fraudulent and unpleasant origins of the [separation] doctrine: "Precisely because of its history—both its lack of constitutional authority and its development in response to [anti-Catholic] prejudice—the idea of separation should, at best, be viewed with suspicion." As constitutional doctrine, the myth should be viewed with contempt. *Separation of Church and State*, to the extent that law and public discourse retain any degree of intellectual integrity, should begin the process of changing our thinking and that of our magistrates. Whether or not this occurs, Hamburger has made a major contribution to historical scholarship.[11]

Tragically, the anti-Catholic and anti-religious sentiments expressed by Black in *Everson* have been carried forward through decision after decision during the past five decades and have poisoned our entire legal system with an anti-Christian bias. As the late Chief Justice William Rehnquist wrote in 1985, the idea of "separation of church and state" as claimed by Justice Black "is a metaphor based on bad history, a metaphor which has proved useless as a guide to judging. It should be frankly and explicitly abandoned."[12]

Justice Hugo Black—presumably driven by his anti-Catholic bias—has imposed upon us an inaccurate reading of Thomas Jefferson's views on church-state relationships. *Everson* poisoned the well of our legal system, and we have been suffering the effects of the toxin ever since.

Atheists and the ACLU Assault the Pledge

Hugo Black's *Everson* ruling has been used as a battering ram to strip our nation of public displays of Christian symbols and any Christian influence in our culture. My mother, Madalyn Murray O'Hair, helped lead this effort long before she founded the American Atheists in 1963. Her ambitious goal was to wipe out every public display of and support for religion in America. Her hatred of belief in God and of America was based upon her belief in Communism as the perfect system of government. Her love of Communism was so complete that she actually tried to move our family to the Soviet Union in 1960, at the height of the cold war.

Writing in a lengthy essay, "The Battle Is Joined," in the *American Atheist* magazine (vol. 33, no. 3), my mother described the objectives of the American Atheists organization. It was to challenge:

> . . . every endorsement of religion by government: the exemption of religion's income from income tax; the Pledge of Allegiance to the flag recited by schoolchildren, particularly

the addition of the words "under God" to the pledge; the statement "In God We Trust" printed on coins and currency of the nation. . . .[13]

She also wanted to ban postage stamps with religious inscriptions on them and cancellation stamps that said, "Pray for Peace"; prohibit Christmas caroling at the Texas State Capitol Rotunda; ban religious courses at the University of Texas; and prohibit "So, help me God" in oaths of office. Her anti-Christian list goes on and on.

My mother filed an unsuccessful lawsuit in 1978 to have "In God We Trust" removed from our currency. The Fifth Circuit U.S. Court of Appeals in Texas ruled against her. The court said the use of "In God We Trust" ". . . is of a patriotic or ceremonial character and bears no true resemblance to a governmental sponsorship of religious exercise." (Even the liberal Ninth Circuit Court came to the same conclusion in 1970 in *Aronow v. United States*.) Her effort failed, but in 1988, American Atheists, headed by my brother Jon Murray, announced it was going to file yet another lawsuit against "In God We Trust" and would also lobby to have this national motto changed to *E Pluribus Unum* ("Out of many, one"). Jon told the Baptist Press at the time, "We're going to keep at it until [laws] are changed, until those public arenas are secular. We want a nation with a government that is completely neutral about religion."

Benevolent Neutrality?

In my book *Let Us Pray*, I devote an entire chapter to my mother's successful campaign to have state-endorsed prayer removed from our nation's public schools. In an 8–1 Supreme Court ruling, the justices decided that children could not recite a prayer each morning before school began.

Justice Tom Clark wrote the majority opinion for the Court, and all other justices except Potter Stewart concurred with him.

Clark and his associates determined prayer violates the First Amendment's ban on laws respecting an establishment of religion. Clark said the government had to remain completely neutral toward religion and that any "breach of neutrality that is today a trickling stream may all too soon become a raging torrent . . ." He then quoted James Madison as saying, ". . . it is proper to take alarm at the first experiment on our liberties."[14] Clark's claim that the government must remain neutral toward religion is based upon a false premise, and this Supreme Court decision simply replaced Christianity with the religion of secular humanism as the dominant religious system in our culture.

The Supreme Court's imposition of secularism upon our culture had been going on for decades before my mother's attack on prayer in the schools, but this case solidified the wall of separation between religion and government.

The justices viewed their imposition of secularism upon our culture as a kind of benevolent neutrality. However, this is false. Secular humanists have their own "values" and they have successfully forced those upon children in our nation's public schools. The "neutrality" allegedly sought by Tom Clark and his associates was not neutrality at all. It was simply a switching of systems of morality, from Christianity to an atheistic humanism that rejects concepts of absolute morality and a Creator who ultimately determines right and wrong.

Senator Rick Santorum (R-PA) wrote to me that he is of the opinion that the modern notion of neutrality toward religion was invented by the justices and is not part of America's history or heritage. Stated Senator Santorum:

The recent efforts to remove the words "under God" from the Pledge of Allegiance, while disturbing, are merely the latest symptom of the Supreme Court's quest for "a strict and lofty neutrality" with regard to religion. Yet never before in our history has America been neutral on religion. Instead, prior to the Everson case in 1947, religion and religious expression were part of the very fabric of our Nation. The neutrality concept is purely an invention of the Court, and America has been living with its consequences ever since.

Recently, the neutrality concept has been used to declare unconstitutional practices like prayer at high school graduation and football games. But the truth is that neutrality is not required by the Constitution of the United States—and the "neutrality" practiced by the Court is, in my belief, not actually neutral at all. What we now have is Court-mandated hostility to religious influence in our society, all in the name of neutrality. Any intellectually and historically honest individual will know that surely, such hostility was never the intent of our Founders.[15]

Franky Schaeffer, writing in his classic, *A Time for Anger: The Myth of Neutrality,* pointed out the disastrous consequences of promoting the bogus idea of neutrality toward religion: "In the guise of advocating 'neutrality,' secular humanists have replaced our nation's set of operating principles . . . and have effectively established secular humanism as the only national religion."[16] The Supreme Court privileged a secular value system, and the Court's stance has continued to be overwhelmingly hostile toward true religion.

Not only has secular humanism become the national religion under the guise of "neutrality," but the "churches" of secular humanism are the public schools—where children are indoctrinated every day and in every class with the doctrines of humanism. Those doctrines include homosexuality, abortion, sexual promiscuity, political liberalism, rationalism (opposition to the idea that God exists), evolution, disrespect for authority or tradition, disrespect for our nation's history and role in the world, globalism, and whatever new fad humanist thinkers come up with along the way.

These values are decidedly anti-Christian and are certainly not part of a neutral worldview. Yet, these values are the ones to which our children are subjected in our public schools—under the guise of protecting children from religious influences!

The Long History of ACLU Hostility toward Christianity

One of the key groups trying to erase every vestige of America's Christian heritage is the ACLU. Since its founding in 1920, the ACLU has been waging war against Christianity. One of its first anti-Christian efforts was to orchestrate a test case to fight for evolution to be taught in public schools. The ACLU advertised for a high school teacher in Tennessee who would teach the theory of evolution in violation of state law. That case came to be known as the "Scopes Monkey Trial," a highly publicized media circus that misrepresented and ridiculed biblical beliefs as ignorant and unscientific. A founder of the ACLU, lawyer Clarence Darrow, was lionized in the press by atheist reporters like H. L. Mencken, who also mercilessly attacked Darrow's Christian opponent, William Jennings Bryan. The whole story of this biased and dishonest event and how it damaged the position of Christianity in American law is related in the excellent book *Monkey Business* by Marvin Olasky and John Perry.[17]

The ACLU's anti-Christian bigotry has continued unabated ever since, and is plainly evident in numerous lawsuits filed over the past few years, including those against the Pledge of Allegiance. The ACLU has not only targeted "under God" as a violation of church-state separation, but opposes state laws that require students to even *hear* the Pledge of Allegiance in school classrooms. The ACLU's apparent hatred of Christianity is so extreme it fights against students having any exposure to "under God" or any references to religion in schools or in public places.

Just in the past few years, the ACLU has done the following:

- In 2003, the ACLU of Pennsylvania filed a federal lawsuit against a state law that requires schools to display the American flag and to offer either the Pledge of Allegiance or the National Anthem for participation by students at the start of each school day. The law didn't force students to say the Pledge or sing the National Anthem, and it gave students' parents the opportunity to opt out if they objected.
- In 2004, the ACLU won a settlement from the state of Colorado over a state law that required students and teachers in public schools to recite the Pledge each morning—with some exceptions. In fact, the ACLU was awarded $91,456 in legal costs after winning the case. (ACLU lawyers are making millions of dollars by bringing these lawsuits and winning court costs.)
- In 2006 in Florida, the ACLU defeated a school system in a case involving a student who refused to stand during the Pledge of Allegiance. The ACLU also won $32,500 in damages and lawyer's fees for this case.

The attacks against the Pledge of Allegiance are not the only efforts being made by the ACLU to strip our nation of its religious heritage. In recent years, the ACLU has launched a campaign to get cities and counties to remove the Ten Commandments from public displays and to force local and state governments to remove any crosses or other Christian symbols from their official seals.

Los Angeles County was one of the largest local governments in the nation to cave to the demands of the ACLU after this anti-Christian group discovered a tiny cross on the county seal. The ACLU sent a letter of concern to the Los Angeles Board of Supervisors about the tiny cross, and the board immediately caved without a fight. Interestingly enough, the ACLU had no objection whatever to another symbol on the seal: an image of the Greek goddess Pomona. Pagan goddesses are okay; Christian symbols are not.[18]

In 1999, the ACLU filed a lawsuit in Missouri on behalf of a Wiccan (a modern practitioner of witchcraft) named Jean Webb who was "offended" by the presence of a fish (a traditional Christian symbol) on the official seal of Republic, Missouri. A federal judge ruled in favor of the ACLU and claimed the fish symbol was unconstitutional because it indicated that Christianity was the official religion of Republic. In his opinion, federal Judge Russell Clark stated: "The portrayal of the fish impermissibly excludes other religious beliefs or non-beliefs and—intended or not—depicts Christianity as the religion endorsed and recognized by the residents of Republic. The Republic city seal pervasively invades the daily lives of non-Christians and sends a message that they are outsiders. The Constitution forbids such a result." According to ACLU leader Eddie Lorenzo, Mrs. Webb "didn't feel comfortable living in a city that endorsed one particular faith over another."[19]

This badly flawed decision and many more like it are the direct result of Justice Black's erroneous reading of Jefferson's statement on the alleged separation of church and state. Black also wrongly imposed his view that the First Amendment was absorbed into the 14th Amendment—thus applying the Bill of Rights to the states, instead of only to the federal government, as intended by the Founding Fathers.

The Fourteenth Amendment does empower the federal government to step in and overrule the states in certain cases where a citizen's civil rights are being violated, as for instance when the voting rights of blacks, along with other rights of citizenship, were denied in some southern states. Yet a great problem arose when the Court wrongly interpreted all manner of religious freedom cases as being civil rights cases. Thus, if the only atheist in town happens to catch sight of a small display of the Ten Commandments on a courthouse lawn, or a small cross on a city seal, he claims his civil rights are being violated. And often the federal courts agree!

An added bonus for the ACLU lawyers is that in civil rights cases the plaintiff's lawyers, if they win, are paid out of the public treasury—and what's more, they get to set their own fees!

I saw up close just how destructive the ACLU tactics of intimidation can be to a community when they launched an attack against the Pontotoc, Mississippi, school district, in a case that took years to wind through the court system. Starting in 1994, I made several trips to Pontotoc; I also brought community leaders to Washington to meet with legislators. In the end, I had to help this small and poor school district, with only 24,000 people in the entire county, raise $144,000 to pay the ACLU lawyers who had bullied and harassed them for so long and finally won in court. What was their crime? They had allowed students to continue a long tradition of leading devotionals over the school intercom. The content of the devotionals was up to the students and did not have to be specifically religious, but they often were, and this upset an atheist mother who had moved her family to town.

Most school districts, to avoid a similar fate, just bend over backward and surrender their First Amendment rights in hopes of staying out of trouble with the courts and the ACLU. After all, even if the school does win, the courts will not award their attorneys any compensation—it will be up to the local district to bear the expenses of a legal battle that could last several years.

The ACLU is targeting Christian religious symbols all over the United States. In San Diego, the ACLU has waged a years-long war against a 43-foot cross on top of the Mount Soledad

War Memorial. After a fifteen-year battle, the ACLU defeated the San Diego City Council.

In 2003, the ACLU filed suit against the National Park Service to remove plaques located around the Grand Canyon and inscribed with Bible verses. The ACLU, however, did not protest the fact that some Grand Canyon buttes were named after Hindu and Egyptian deities: Brahma Temple, Vishnu Temple, Shiva Temple, Osiris Temple, and others.

The ACLU, of course, has been involved in numerous court cases to have displays of the Ten Commandments removed from public buildings.

The most famous Ten Commandments cases in recent years involve the public display of the Decalogue on public buildings in Kentucky and on the State Capitol grounds in Austin, Texas. The Kentucky case involved the posting of the Ten Commandments on two county courthouses. The ACLU sued to have the Ten Commandments removed. Instead of caving to the bullying tactics of the ACLU, the counties then added eight other historical documents to the display to show the influence of religion in the founding of our nation. The ACLU was still not satisfied and a federal court ordered a ban on the displays.[20]

The county officials then changed the display to make it a "Foundation of American Law and Government Display," thinking this would give it a secular purpose that would satisfy the ACLU and the federal judge. This display included words from "The Star Spangled Banner," the Declaration of Independence, and other patriotic or legal documents. Of course, the federal judge and ACLU still ruled it had specific Christian content, which violated the alleged separation of church and state.

The Supreme Court heard this case (*McCreary County v. ACLU*) in 2005, and Justice David Souter wrote the majority (5–4) opinion against the "Foundation of American Law and Government Display." According to Souter, this display was simply a "sham" designed to hide the religious purpose behind it. Thus, it violated the "establishment clause" of the Constitution.[21]

In the Texas case, heard and decided on the same days as *McCreary County*, the Supreme Court was to determine whether a six-foot historical monument of the Ten Commandments on the Texas State Capitol grounds was constitutional. The monument had been donated by the Fraternal Order of Eagles and had stood on the Capitol grounds for 40 years. Disbarred lawyer Thomas Van Orden filed suit against the monument, claiming he was "offended" whenever he saw it. Van Orden, at the time, was homeless and lived in a tent. He regularly visited the State Law Library just to have a warm place to stay. The media dubbed Van Orden "the homeless lawyer," but he had his law license suspended in 1985 for taking money from clients for work he failed to perform. He claimed to be a "religious pluralist" and joined the Unitarian Church, but seldom attended services.

During his walks to the State Law Library, he noticed the Ten Commandments monument and decided to challenge the display in court. He contacted left-wing Duke University law professor Erwin Chemerinsky about his proposed lawsuit and the professor agreed to take the case for free. Fortunately, Chemerinsky eventually lost.[22]

In this case (*Van Orden v. Perry*), the Supreme Court ruled 5–4 that the Ten Commandments monument was constitutional. Why was this monument constitutional when the Kentucky display was not? Chief Justice William Rehnquist wrote (quoting *Lynch v. Donnelly* [1984]), "There is an unbroken history of official acknowledgment by all three branches of government of the role of religion in American life from at least 1789," and that this monument reflected that tradition. Justices John Stevens and Ruth Bader Ginsburg, two of the most liberal judges on the Supreme Court, dissented and claimed the monument was an impermissible endorsement of monotheism by the state of Texas! Stevens wrote that the display of this monument would make nonmonotheists and nonbelievers "feel like [outsiders] in matters of faith, and [strangers] in the political community."[23] During oral arguments in the Texas case, Justice Antonin Scalia sparred with Chemerinsky over the legality of displaying the Ten Commandments monument. Justice Scalia told Chemerinsky:

> It [the Ten Commandments monument] is a profound religious message, but it's a profound religious message believed in by the vast majority of the American people, just as belief in monotheism is shared by a vast majority of the American people. And our traditions show that there is nothing wrong with the government reflecting that. I mean, we're a tolerant society religiously, but just as the majority has to be tolerant of minority views, in matters of religion, it seems to me that the minority has to be tolerant of the majority's ability to express its belief that government comes from God, which is what this is about.[24]

Chemerinsky disagreed, claiming such displays make "some individuals feel like outsiders."

Stephen B. Presser, Raoul Berger Professor of Legal History at Northwestern University School of Law, analyzed the Kentucky and Texas cases in *The American Spectator* in October 2005. Presser wrote that these two cases show how confused the Supreme Court is over its various religious freedom decisions—and how arbitrary are its decisions. Presser wrote:

> A lot of strange stuff has been coming from the United States Supreme Court lately, but for sheer incoherence nothing beats the Court's "establishment clause" jurisprudence. ... Original understanding [of the Constitution] can't clear up everything in constitutional law, but if the Court were more committed to interpreting the Constitution

rather than social planning for the Republic, it might well diminish the number of 5–4 decisions rendered on important public issues.[25]

The Kentucky and Texas cases show what a confusing legal quagmire the Supreme Court has created by its slavish adherence to the wrongly decided *Everson* case. These cases also demonstrate the way radical individuals and organizations are using badly decided court cases to rewrite history, undermine morality, and remove any influence of Christianity from public life. They are also using these cases to institutionalize the concept that an "offended" individual has the constitutional right to veto the freedom of religion or speech of millions of Americans.

Alliance Defense Fund attorney Jordan Lorence described this "offended" individual idea in an editorial in *WorldNetDaily* in February 2005, before the Kentucky and Texas cases were decided by the Supreme Court. Lorence urged the Supreme Court to use these two cases to clearly reject the "offended observer" idea as having no legal merit.

According to Lorence, the Supreme Court has repeatedly rejected the "offended observer" idea as one that has no validity. In the rejection of Michael Newdow's first lawsuit against "under God" in the Pledge, Justice Sandra Day O'Connor said: "The Constitution does not guarantee citizens a right entirely to avoid ideas with which they disagree. . . . No robust democracy insulates its citizens from views that they might find novel or even inflammatory."[26] Yet, according to Lorence, the ACLU claimed in its Kentucky lawsuit against the public display of the Ten Commandments that its clients "perceive this Ten Commandments display as a violation of the Constitution. . . . Each plaintiff therefore is offended by the continued display." In writing on the Kentucky and Texas cases, Lorence correctly observes:

The fact that the government and not a private individual presents the offensive message should not empower offended observers to silence the government. Someone will always object to any government message—"support our troops," "just say no to drugs" or "liberty and justice for all." Being offended by walking by a message passively displayed does not demonstrate that someone has suffered actual concrete harm by the government's actions. And a passive display certainly does not constitute an "establishment of religion" because it does not compel anyone to do anything. The Supreme Court should take the opportunity offered by the Ten Commandments cases to shut down the "offended observer" aberration in the law and stop these secularist "hecklers" from vetoing governmental acknowledgments of our nation's faith-based heritage.[27]

Yet if the federal courts—including the Supreme Court—are not restricted from ruling on such issues as the Pledge of Allegiance, even worse decisions will begin to emerge from the minds of liberal activist judges prompted by legal briefs created by ACLU lawyers, Michael Newdow, and other enemies of Christianity.

What's Next: The Declaration of Independence Banned as Unconstitutional?

The extent of church-state separation anxiety among some paranoid school officials has become so absurd that in 2004, the principal of Stevens Creek School in Cupertino, California, actually began requiring fifth-grade history teacher Stephen Williams to submit all his lesson plans to her. Why? Because in teaching history, Williams included supplementary materials that included: the Declaration of Independence; excerpts from the diaries of John Adams and George Washington; the writings of William Penn; several state constitutions; "The Rights of Colonists" by Samuel Adams; and a fact sheet on the history of "In God We Trust" on our nation's coins and paper currency.

Principal Patricia Vidmar rejected any of Williams' lesson plans or reference materials that included statements about God or Christianity in our nation's history! Not to be intimidated by his uninformed principal, Williams contacted the Alliance Defense Fund (ADF), and this religious freedom group agreed to defend his right to use historical documents (with religious references) to teach American history.

In April 2005, the ADF won a legal victory in this case when a federal judge ruled that Williams' lawsuit has merit and could proceed. In the legal brief filed by the ADF on behalf of Williams, it documented the various discussions that were taking place in his history class, including a discussion of "under God" in the Pledge of Allegiance and *The Lion, the Witch, and the Wardrobe* by C. S. Lewis.

In his assignments, Williams often sent supplementary materials home with the students for them to study on their own. Principal Vidmar was clearly outraged by this action and sent him a memo, which said, in part:

> I . . . am, hereby, directing you to stop sending out materials of a religious nature with your students. I am directing you to provide me with an "advance" copy of materials you will be sending home at least two days prior to their being sent out so I can make sure that the materials will not be of concern to the parents or violate the separation of religion from public education.[28]

Vidmar's last sentence may reveal more than she wanted about her attitudes about religion and education. She obviously believes public schools are to be religion-free zones. In her mind, even the Declaration of Independence and the other writings of the founders are off-limits because they mention God. How can one accurately teach American history without mentioning the overwhelming role that the Christian religion played in the founding of this nation? This is church-state separation anxiety taken to a whole new level. Is the Declaration of Independence now unconstitutional? Even the Constitution mentions God by referencing "the year of our Lord." Will some clever ACLU lawyer or some renegade federal judge on the Ninth Circuit Court argue that the Constitution itself is unconstitutional because it contains the word "Lord"?

Just how ridiculous can this myth of church-state separation become? Well, there are predictions that the ACLU, in its cases against crosses on city seals and on public property, is actually setting up a legal history for claiming that the names of cities such as Los Angeles (City of Angels) violate the separation of church and state!

Joerg Knipprath, a professor of constitutional law at Southwestern University School of Law in Los Angeles, thinks this could be the next logical step the ACLU takes. Will the ACLU target Los Angeles's name? "That's absolutely right," Knipprath told the *Los Angeles Daily News* (June 13, 2004). "The cross is a minor symbol on the county seal whereas Los Angeles is the 'City of Angels.' San Clemente, Santa Monica, Sacramento, San Francisco, etc., are all religious references. . . . It's far-fetched at this point. I don't think it's going to happen in the next ten years. But if somebody said ten or twenty years ago that we were going to challenge the Pledge of Allegiance or this tiny little cross on the county seal, the argument would have been that was far-fetched, too." I predict this will come far sooner than ten years from now.[29]

Douglas Kmiec, a constitutional law professor at Pepperdine University, agrees. He told the *Los Angeles Daily News*: "The logic of the ACLU's reasoning would suggest that Santa

Monica should be renamed Monica, San Diego should be renamed Diego and on down the line. Los Angeles is a similar reference to angels. The full title of Los Angeles is a distinctly religious name." (The full title of Los Angeles is: "The Town of Our Lady the Queen of Angels of the Little Portion.")[30]

The Attack on the Pledge:
Part of an Overall Anti-Christian Agenda

As we have seen, the assaults on the Pledge of Allegiance are not isolated cases of "offended observers" attempting to seek redress for actual injuries to them. The legal attacks against the Pledge are part of a nationwide, coordinated effort headed by the ACLU and militant atheists like Michael Newdow to change our culture and government into a single secularized, godless entity.

Protecting the Pledge and "under God" is just one battle in this overall war against Christianity and all moral laws based upon the Bible. The atheists and ACLU radicals are subverting the foundations upon which our nation was founded—and if they succeed, they will have destroyed the very principles that give us representative government, and freedom of speech and religion. Once this is achieved, laws will be based upon the ever-changing whims of liberal judges and legislators—not upon God's never-changing moral laws as given to us in the Old and New Testaments. In a godless America, we could eventually face the kind of society envisioned by George Orwell in *1984*. In it, the tortured Winston Smith is told by the evil character O'Brien: "If you want a vision of the future, Winston, imagine a boot stamping on a human face forever." This kind of society is without our merciful God as the Lawgiver.

CHAPTER 7

Judicial Activism
And the Pledge

ATHEIST Michael Newdow always seems to be offended by public displays of religious belief. He is offended by the coins and paper currency that bear the inscription "In God We Trust." He was offended by President Bush's inauguration in 2001 because the President invited Evangelist Franklin Graham and Pastor Kirbyjon Caldwell to deliver Christian invocations. And, most of all, Newdow claims to have been offended by his daughter reciting "under God" each day in a California elementary school. His daughter, who is a devout Christian, enjoyed saying the Pledge, but Newdow claimed before the Supreme Court he was being psychologically injured by her recitation.

Newdow, who is a lawyer and emergency room physician, is perpetually offended by Christianity and has admitted he wants to wipe out all government acknowledgments of religious belief in our nation.

This atheist is attempting to concoct a new "right" under our Constitution: the "right" not to be offended. He is finding friends in our federal courts who agree with him.

Newdow Finds New Friends in the Ninth Circuit Court of Appeals

Michael Newdow has made international headlines over his lawsuit against the Pledge of Allegiance. He first filed his lawsuit against "under God" in the Pledge in March 2000 in a federal district court in California. His case was directed against the Elk Grove Unified School District, where his daughter attended school. In his lawsuit, he claimed, even though she was not required to recite the Pledge, she was still compelled to "watch and listen as her state-employed teacher in her state-run school leads her classmates in a ritual proclaiming that . . . our's [*sic*] is 'one nation under God' " (Perry A. Zinkel, "Courtside: Under God?" *Phi Delta Kappan*, 84, no. 10, [2003]).

A lower court dismissed his case in July 2000 but he persisted, and the Ninth Circuit Court of Appeals issued its decision declaring the Pledge unconstitutional on June 26, 2002. Writing for the majority, Judge Alfred T. Goodwin wrote: "A profession that we are a nation 'under God' is identical, for establishment-clause purposes, to a profession that we are a nation under Jesus, a nation under Vishnu, a nation under Zeus or a nation under no god because none of these professions can be neutral with respect to religion." The court also said, "The coercive effect of this policy is particularly pronounced in the school setting given the age and impressionability of schoolchildren, and their understanding that they are required to adhere to the norms set by their school, their teacher and their fellow students."[1]

The court sided with Newdow in the bogus claim that just "hearing" the Pledge being recited is coercive and violates the alleged separation of church and state.

Newdow explained why he sued to have "under God" removed from the Pledge in the Winter 2002 issue of *Free Inquiry*, a humanist magazine. He portrayed atheists as victims of discrimination in a religious society and declared that his crusade against the Pledge was a "civil rights campaign, as important and as serious as any in our history."[2]

Newdow compared his campaign against the Pledge to the civil rights movement and the feminist movement. According to Newdow, "We greatly improved our society when we altered our laws to stop encouraging racial segregation, barring women from the workplace, and ignoring the disabled. The goal of the Pledge lawsuit is only to attain further improvement."[3]

Newdow Exploits His Christian Daughter

Newdow's unethical use of his daughter is a story that needs to be widely known. When Newdow filed his lawsuit—allegedly to protect his daughter from hearing the Pledge of Allegiance—he had no legal authority over her. He had never married Sandy Banning, the mother of their daughter, and Ms. Banning had full legal custody.

In fact, Sandy Banning has publicly stated her daughter enjoyed saying the Pledge and that both are devout Christians. Ms. Banning's opposition to Newdow's efforts is so strong that she established the One Nation Under God Foundation for the specific purpose of defending the Pledge of Allegiance from her ex-partner's atheistic efforts (Charles Lane, "U.S. Court to Bar Pledge of Allegiance; Use of 'God' Called Unconstitutional," *The Washington Post*, 6/27/2002, Section A).

Ninth Circuit Court Decision Wrongly Decided

The anti-Pledge decision issued by the Ninth Circuit Court was appealed to the U.S. Supreme Court. The high court disputed the Ninth's reasoning and overturned the decision on June 14, 2004.

Nearly two dozen congressmen filed a friend-of-the-court brief to defend the Pledge against the Ninth Circuit Court and

Michael Newdow. The brief included my good friend Congressman Todd Akin (R-MO), who two years later sponsored the Pledge Protection Act of 2006.

The brief was filed by the American Center for Law and Justice (ACLJ) and contains some compelling arguments in defense of the Pledge of Allegiance and "under God." It also has a devastating critique of Michael Newdow and his fraudulent claim of "harm" from his daughter reciting the Pledge. In this brief, the ACLJ says:

> The Ninth Circuit's judgment should be vacated, and the matter remanded with instructions to return it to the district court for dismissal because the court lacked jurisdiction over Newdow's claims. As a non-custodial parent with no decision-making authority over his daughter's education, Newdow had no Article III standing to be in federal court. Newdow's alleged injury was not "distinct" and "palpable," as required by this Court's precedents, and he suffered no invasion of any legally protectable interest. Upon learning of Newdow's legal relationship with his daughter, the only right the Ninth Court could identify was Newdow's supposed right to have his child shielded in public school from religious views that differ from his own. A right of such magnitude has stunning implications for the future relationship between the federal judiciary and public education. The Ninth Circuit's ruling encourages disenchanted parents whose religious feelings are similarly offended by what their children are taught in public schools to clog federal court dockets with litigation.
>
> In fact, Newdow's alleged injury is nothing more than psychological offense at the historical fact that this Nation was founded upon a belief in monotheism, and that the Pledge of Allegiance reflects that fact. Psychological offense alone does not suffice to confer Article III standing.[4]

Michael Newdow represented himself before the U.S. Supreme Court in this case. To the surprise of many conservatives, even the more liberal justices on the Court were skeptical about Newdow's claims of injury due to his daughter reciting the Pledge each morning.

Justice Stephen Breyer, for example, indicated to Newdow that he thought the phrase "under God" was simply "ceremonial deism" and could be acceptable. Justice David Souter opined that, "I think the argument is that simply the way we live and think and work in schools and in civic society in which the Pledge is made, that the—that whatever is distinctly religious as an affirmation is simply lost." According to Souter, reciting the Pledge is just a way of "solemnizing" an occasion.[5]

Newdow objected to this reasoning and continued to maintain that the Pledge was coercive because it forced students to listen to an affirmation of God in public school. According to Newdow: "I am an atheist. I don't believe in God. And every school morning my child is asked to stand up, face that flag, put her hand over her heart and say that her father is wrong. . . . That is an actual, concrete, discrete, particularized, individualized harm to me."[6]

During Newdow's debate with the justices, Sandra Day O'Connor asked him if he objected to "In God We Trust" on U.S. currency. Newdow responded: "Only if my daughter is forced to say, 'In God We Trust.'" Newdow was being dishonest when he said this, as we will see.

During oral arguments, the Supreme Court also heard from Terence Cassidy, a lawyer for the Elk Grove School District and from Theodore B. Olson, the solicitor general of the United States.

Cassidy correctly argued that Newdow had no legal standing to bring the Pledge lawsuit in the first place because he had no custodial authority over his daughter.[7]

Olson argued, also correctly, that "fourteen justices of this court since the Pledge of Allegiance was amended have indicated that the Pledge of Allegiance is not a religious exercise. It is something different, of a ceremonial nature." In addition, said Olson:

> The [Constitution] does not prohibit civic and ceremonial acknowledgments of the indisputable historical fact of the religious heritage that caused the Framers of our Constitution and the signers of the Declaration of Independence to say that they had the right to revolt and start a new country, because although the king was infallible, they believed that God gave them the right to declare their independence when the king has not been living up to the unalienable principles given to them by God.[8]

During this part of the debate Justice Ruth Bader Ginsburg asked Olson if he would support the Pledge if it included "under Jesus." Olson responded: "That is completely different. The Founders, said Olson, referred to the deity as Creator but did not refer to Jesus Christ in their founding documents.

The ACLJ friend-of-the-court brief also pointed out that the Pledge accurately reflects the historical facts surrounding the founding of this nation and the strongly held belief among the Founding Fathers that God was the author of our liberties—not governments or a British king. The brief stated:

> The Founders of this Nation based a national philosophy on a belief in Deity. The Declaration of Independence and the Bill of Rights locate inalienable rights in a Creator rather than in government, precisely so that such rights cannot be stripped away by government. In 1782, Thomas Jefferson wrote, "Can the liberties of a nation be thought secure when we have removed their only firm basis, a conviction in the minds of the people that these liberties are the gift of God? That they are not to be violated but with His wrath?"[9]

The Father of the Country, George Washington, acknowledged on many occasions the role of Divine Providence
in the Nation's affairs. His first inaugural address is replete
with references to God, including thanksgivings and sup-
plications. In Washington's Proclamation of a Day of
National Thanksgiving, he wrote that it is the "duty of all
nations to acknowledge the providence of Almighty God,
to obey His will, to be grateful for His benefits, and
humbly to implore His protection and favor. . . . George
Washington used the phrase "under God" in several of his
orders to the Continental Army. On one occasion he
wrote that "The fate of unborn millions will now depend,
under God, on the courage and conduct of this army."
The Founders may have differed over the contours of the
relationship between religion and government, but they
never deviated from the conviction that "there was a necessary and valuable moral connection between the two."
Philip Hamburger, *Separation of Church and State* 480
[2002].[10]

The ACLJ brief also points out that if the Newdow theory
of "offense" takes root in our legal system, it will clog the courts
of our nation with individuals offended about all sorts of things
in our public schools or in the culture at large.

The ACLJ brief also warns:

Equally disturbing is the likelihood that a decision affirm-
ing the Ninth Circuit will eventually foreclose the
Nation's school districts from teaching students to sing
and appreciate the Nation's patriotic music as well as a
vast universe of classical music with religious themes. Students might learn about the Nation's founding documents
without being required to recite them. Public school
music programs cannot exist, however, without student

performance. Thus, patriotic anthems, such as *America the Beautiful,* and *God Bless America,* will become taboo because they cannot realistically be learned unless they are sung. Such musical treasures as Bach's choral arrangements and African-American spirituals will also become constitutionally suspect, at least as part of public school music curricula.[11]

According to the Ninth Circuit's logic, if a group of students sings *God Bless America,* the Establishment Clause is violated because an atheistic student might *feel coerced* to sing along (and indeed may well be coerced inasmuch as music teachers are not constitutionally compelled to exempt students from singing with the class). . . .

An affirmance of the Ninth Circuit's decision will threaten a sort of Orwellian reformation of public school curricula by censoring American history and excluding much that is valuable in the world of choral music.[12]

The Knights of Columbus filed a friend-of-the-court brief against Newdow and the Ninth Circuit Court. In it, the Knights of Columbus observed:

If reciting the Pledge of Allegiance is now suddenly unconstitutional because it refers to a nation "under God," then reciting the Declaration of Independence, which similarly refers to the Creator as the source of our rights, must at least be suspect. That turns the American theory of rights exactly on its head. To affirm the decision [Ninth Circuit] . . . would be to impose, by order of the Judicial Branch, a drastic change in our national ethos. Instead, the Judicial Branch should respect not only that ethos, but the consistent interpretation of the Establishment Clause reflected in the expression and conduct of both coordinate branches.[13]

American Atheists File Friend-of-the-Court Brief on Newdow Case

The militant atheist group founded by my mother, Madalyn Murray O'Hair, also filed a friend-of-the-court brief in the Michael Newdow case. In the introductory remarks to their brief, they point out the following: "American Atheists' perspective is rooted in the philosophy of materialism, 'which holds that nothing exists but natural phenomenon' [quoting from my mother's writings]. No gods, no spirits, fairies, or other imagined entities pull at the strings of humanity. The materialist philosophy of Atheism promotes a positive viewpoint and provides the impetus to effect change." American Atheists also proclaimed in their Michael Newdow brief that the inclusion of "under God" in the Pledge of Allegiance was "the undisguised attack on Atheism and its materialist philosophy." The introduction quotes my mother at length on atheism and its supposed benefits to society:

> Materialism liberates us, teaches us not to hope for happiness beyond the grave but to prize life on earth and strive always to improve it. Materialism restores to man his dignity and his intellectual integrity. Man is not a worm condemned to crawl in the dust, but a human being capable of mastering the forces of nature and making them serve him. Materialism compels faith in the human intellect, in the power of knowledge of man's ability to fathom all the secrets of nature and to create a social system based upon reason and justice. Materialism has faith in man and his ability to transform the world by his own efforts. It is a philosophy in every essence optimistic, life asserting, and radiant. It considers the struggle for progress a moral obligation, and impossible without noble ideals that inspire men to struggle, to perform bold, creative work."[14]

In reality, atheistic materialism was the foundational philosophy of the Soviet Union and Communist China, where multiplied millions of individuals were slaughtered for opposing tyranny. The noble ideals of materialism she speaks so highly of resulted in the Soviet gulags and the Chinese laogai slave labor camps for religious and political dissidents. Her claim that atheists wish to found a culture based on reason and justice reminds me of the French Revolution, where the "Goddess of Reason" was worshipped in the Cathedral of Notre Dame in Paris in 1793, at the same time the guillotine became the bloody symbol of a country run by militant atheists.

The Supreme Court Rules against Ninth Circuit Opinion

Despite the best efforts of the atheists and the ACLU lawyers, on June 14, 2004 (Flag Day and the 50th Anniversary of the 1954 vote adding "under God" to the Pledge), the Supreme Court issued a ruling against the Ninth Circuit Court and Michael Newdow. The Court ruled that Newdow had no legal standing to bring the lawsuit in the first place—something the ACLJ and other conservative legal scholars had argued all along.

Supreme Court Justice Stephen Breyer wrote the majority opinion for the Court. After reviewing all of the facts of the case, including Newdow's noncustodial parent status, he concluded: ". . . Newdow lacks prudential standing to bring this suit in federal court."[15] Chief Justice William Rehnquist, in a concurring opinion, wrote, "I do not believe that the phrase 'under God' in the Pledge converts its recital into a 'religious exercise' . . . Instead, it is a declaration of belief in allegiance and loyalty to the United States flag and the Republic that it represents. The phrase 'under God' is in no sense a prayer, nor an endorsement of any religion, but a simple recognition of the fact" that America was founded on a fundamental belief in God.

Justice William Rehnquist also noted: "The Constitution only requires that schoolchildren be entitled to abstain from the [Pledge] ceremony if they chose to do so. To give the parent of such a child a sort of 'heckler's veto' over a patriotic ceremony willingly participated in by other students, simply because the Pledge of Allegiance contains the descriptive phrase, 'under God,' is an unwarranted extension of the Establishment Clause, an extension which would have the unfortunate effect of prohibiting a commendable patriotic observance."[16]

Justice Sandra Day O'Connor agreed with Rehnquist in this decision and stated:

> Michael Newdow's challenge to petitioner school district's policy is a well-intentioned one, but his distaste for the reference to "one Nation under God," however sincere, cannot be the yardstick of our Establishment Clause inquiry. Certain ceremonial references to God and religion in our Nation are the inevitable consequences of the religious history that gave birth to our founding principles of liberty. It would be ironic indeed, if this Court were to wield our constitutional commitment to religious freedom so as to sever our ties to the traditions developed to honor it.[17]

Michael Newdow lost this case on a technicality—the ruling that he had no legal standing to bring it. This allowed him to bring the issue before the courts again. And he did not give up. In 2005, Newdow found a group of parents in California with children in public school who claim to be offended by the Pledge of Allegiance, and he has filed a new lawsuit on their behalf that is on its way to the Supreme Court.

Ninth Circuit Judge Lawrence Karlton, an appointee of President Jimmy Carter, ruled in Newdow's favor in the second lawsuit. Karlton claimed he was bound by the "precedent" of the previous Ninth Circuit Court ruling in Newdow's first lawsuit.

How a ruling that was tossed out by the Supreme Court can still be considered a binding precedent is a mystery to anyone with a logical mind. Nevertheless, our nation is again facing the possibility that Newdow will succeed in his effort to have "under God" removed from the Pledge of Allegiance.

If Newdow fails at the Supreme Court level, it is almost inevitable that the ACLU or Americans United for Separation of Church and State will find more "offended" atheists who will file similar lawsuits at the state level and those cases will also make their way into federal courts and eventually to the U.S. Supreme Court. The battle over the Pledge could well continue for decades if the Pledge Protection Act of 2006 or a similar law is not passed by Congress and signed into law.

Newdow Continues His Assault Against Religious Liberty

The anti-Christian Newdow isn't content with only removing "under God" from the Pledge. He has vowed to wage a campaign to remove "In God We Trust" from our coins and is determined to get a federal court to rule against letting pastors participate in presidential ceremonies.

Newdow announced his campaign against "In God We Trust" in a federal lawsuit filed in November 2005. In this case, his lawsuit is against the United States Congress for its authorization of the inscription on our currency in 1955. Newdow's 162-page brief claims, "The placement of 'In God We Trust' on the coins and currency was clearly done for religious purposes and to have religious effects."[18]

In 2004, Newdow filed a lawsuit in U.S. District Court for the District of Columbia to bar the use of clergy during presidential events. Newdow's lawsuit claims, "It is an offense of the highest magnitude that the leader of our nation, while swearing to uphold the Constitution, publicly violates that very document upon taking his oath of office."[19]

Newdow was offended by the fact that President Bush invited two clergymen to give invocations during his inauguration in 2001. According to Newdow, such prayers turn non-Christians "into second-class citizens and create division on the basis of religion."[20]

Newdow will undoubtedly continue to file frivolous lawsuits in various federal court jurisdictions throughout the country. Along the way he will also likely find liberal activist and anti-Christian judges who will be more willing to accommodate his objectives of cleansing our nation of its Christian heritage and symbols.

Restrain the Ninth Circuit Court and Liberal Judges!

Michael Newdow's radical atheism has become a significant threat to religious freedom in America, but a far more serious problem involves the willingness of activist liberal judges to ignore the Constitution and America's Christian history when they issue rulings on the Pledge or other religious freedom issues.

The radical left-wing judges on the Ninth Circuit Court in San Francisco are prime examples of an out-of-control judiciary. As of this writing, the Ninth Circuit is one of the most extremely liberal federal court systems in the United States and it is by far the most often overturned by the Supreme Court (http://www.onenewsnow.com/2007/03/ninth_circuit_justices_blasted.php).

The Ninth Circuit is the largest federal court system in America in terms of both area and population. It covers the states of California, Washington, Arizona, Alaska, Hawaii, Idaho, Montana, Nevada, and Oregon, as well as Guam and the

Northern Marianas Islands. It has jurisdiction over 56 million Americans and more than 1.3 million square miles of land. Its bad rulings impact the lives of one out of every ten Americans.

The Ninth Circuit Court's record of being overturned by the Supreme Court is a national scandal that must be dealt with by the American people and Congress.

Between 1990 and 1996, the U.S. Supreme Court struck down 73 percent of the Ninth's rulings, while other federal courts averaged only 46 percent reversals. In 1997, the Supreme Court overturned twenty-seven out of twenty-eight of the Ninth's decisions. Between 1996 and 1999, the Ninth was over-turned in fifty-four out of sixty-three cases, for a reversal rate of 86 percent![21] As you can see, it's getting worse and worse.

It is clear there is something fundamentally wrong with the ideologies of the men and women who wear the black robes on the Ninth Circuit. An investigative report published by *Insight on the News* magazine in March 2002 detailed the aggressive left-wing activist mentality of many of the judges on the Ninth Circuit.

The *Insight* report, for example, pointed out that of the twenty-six active judges on the Ninth Circuit in 2002, fourteen were appointed by Bill Clinton and three by Jimmy Carter. President Carter, during his four-year term, managed to appoint fifteen out of twenty-three Ninth Circuit judges who served in the late 1970s and into the 1980s. And the history of the Ninth since at least the 1970s has been one of ruling for the extreme versus the mainstream.

Insight interviewed a former law clerk who had worked with judges on the Ninth Circuit. In his view, reversal by the Supreme Court "is almost a badge of honor to some judges in the Ninth." He observed: "The operating assumption is that all but a fraction of its cases will not be corrected by the Supreme Court, especially on immigration" (http://www.findarticles.com/p/

articles/mi_m1571/is_11_18/ai_84184980/pg_2). Bad cases slip through the cracks, "So you have judges that are flagrantly ignoring Supreme Court precedent because the high court just doesn't have the time to review all the cases."[22]

In 2002, even the extremely liberal Harvard Law Professor Lawrence Tribe warned members of a Senate committee that America could be seriously embarrassed internationally if the Ninth Circuit Court were to become involved in a case involving suspected terrorists. If Lawrence Tribe is worried about the decisions coming from the Ninth, we are in serious trouble.

One of the most prolific and ideologically driven judges on the Ninth Circuit is Stephen Reinhardt. Judge Reinhardt is the fifth husband of Ramona Ripston, who heads the American Civil Liberties Union chapter for Southern California.

Reinhardt, a Carter appointee, was awarded this key position on the federal court probably as a reward for his role as an activist in the Democratic National Committee (DNC). Reinhardt helped engineer the nomination of Carter to the presidency in 1976. In 1979, Carter gave him this plum appointment on the Ninth Circuit. Fox News commentator and former judge Andrew Napolitano has characterized Reinhardt as "probably the most open, notorious, leftist of all the federal judges in the United States."[23]

Reinhardt is one of two judges on a three-judge panel who ruled in 2002 that the Pledge of Allegiance was unconstitutional. Judge Alfred T. Goodwin wrote the opinion for the panel. Judge Ferdinand F. Fernandez, appointed by President George H. W. Bush, was the lone dissenter in the Pledge case. In his dissent, he said there was only a "miniscule" risk that the phrase "under God" would "bring about a theocracy or suppress someone's beliefs."

Reinhardt's radical left-wing views are reflected in most of his other decisions as well. In the past, he has ruled:

- A Mexican doctor who killed a U.S. Drug Enforcement Administration official should not have been forcibly returned to the United States to face prosecution.
- Arizona had no right to mandate English as the official language of the government because the legislation was allegedly "overbroad" and violated the First Amendment.
- The use of police dogs to track down criminals or drugs violated the Fourth Amendment's protection against unreasonable search and seizures.[24]

In addition, Reinhardt has expressed the view that abortion and assisted suicide are both fundamental rights under the Constitution in several rulings. As expected, Reinhardt is a disciple of the "Living Constitution" theory that gives federal judges the ability to redefine the Constitution into whatever they want it to be at any particular moment. Reinhardt calls his belief system "an expansive approach to jurisprudence." I would call it judicial tyranny. Reinhardt is one of the most prolific—and thus one of the most dangerous—federal court judges in America. He regularly participates in an average of 500 cases a year!

In November 2005, Reinhardt and his three-judge panel ruled parents had no right to protest the teaching of sexually explicit subjects to their children in public schools. The case involved parents who protested against their children being given a sex survey in the first, third, and fifth grades. The survey asked these young children if they thought about such things as:

- Touching my private parts too much.
- Having sex.
- Touching other people's private parts.
- Washing myself because I feel dirty on the inside.
- Not trusting people because they might want sex.

Six parents filed a lawsuit against the school district, claiming the district had violated their right to privacy and their right to control the upbringing of their children.

What was Judge Reinhardt's decision? He ruled: "We . . . hold that there is no fundamental right of parents to be the exclusive provider of information regarding sexual matters to their children, either independent of their right to direct the upbringing and education of their children or encompassed by it." Reinhardt further asserted: "As with all constitutional rights, the right of parents to make decisions concerning the care, custody, and control of their children is not without limitations. . . . Schools cannot be expected to accommodate the personal, moral, or religious concerns of every parent."[25]

Of course, Judge Reinhardt is eager to make schools "accommodate the religious (or nonreligious) concerns" of an atheist parent such as Michael Newdow.

Judge Reinhardt rejected the claims of the parents who objected to sexual questions being posed to their young children that their (the parents') right to privacy had been violated, but then went into a defense of such "rights to privacy" as: the "right" to abortion on demand; and the "right" of homosexuals to engage in sodomy.

Reinhardt then said: "We cannot overstate the significance of these rights. They symbolize the importance of our evolving understanding of the nature of our Constitution. (See Stephen G. Breyer, *Active Liberty: Interpreting Our Democratic Constitution* [2005].)[26]

It is significant to note that Reinhardt used Associate Supreme Court Justice Breyer's book to justify his willingness to reject parental rights in favor of the school forcing children to answer sex surveys. Breyer is an advocate of the "Living Constitution" theory of jurisprudence, which gives federal judges a blank check to freely redefine the Constitution to suit their own political biases.

In discussing this outrageous violation of parental rights on *The O'Reilly Factor,* Judge Andrew Napolitano characterized Reinhardt's decision this way: "He said no [to parental rights] in a way that made him sound like Joe Stalin because he basically said the rights of the state trump the rights of the parents."

Host Bill O'Reilly asked Napolitano if it is right to have such an ideologically driven judge on the federal bench. The judge replied: "It's wrong when you have such a committed ideologue who really can't see the other side. That's unfair."[27]

Judge Napolitano was being far too kind when he described Reinhardt's place on the federal bench as "unfair." It is far more than unfair. It is a national scandal. Out-of-control judges like Reinhardt threaten not only parental rights, but the very idea of self-government in the Republic.

Judge Robert Bork, a wonderful advocate of judicial restraint, calls men like Reinhardt "robed masters" and "judicial oligarchs"—men who rule without regard for the original intent of the Constitution or the laws they are called upon to interpret (http://www.firstthings.com/article.php3?id_article=3946).

Are We Ruled by Judges or by Laws?

As we have seen, Michael Newdow poses a major threat to religious freedom in our nation, but he could not do his dirty work without the help of renegade liberal judges on the federal bench!

Judge Robert Bork and Attorney Mark Levin have written scathing critiques of liberal judges who view themselves as above the law. Judge Bork's latest book, *Coercing Virtue: The Worldwide Rule of Judges,* warns of a new trend in legal thinking among liberal judges: the use of foreign court decisions in issuing rulings involving American law and its citizens.

Judge Bork has been sounding the alarm about judicial activists for decades. In 1996, for example, he wrote a devastating critique of the Supreme Court for the journal *First Things.*

In it, Bork described Supreme Court justices this way: "[They] are our masters in a way that no President, Congressman, governor, or other elected official is. They order our lives and we have no recourse, no means of resisting, no means of altering their ukases. They are indeed robed masters."[28]

Attorney Mark Levin, writing in *Men in Black: How the Supreme Court Is Destroying America*, surveyed the damage the Supreme Court has done to our nation's morality, national security, educational system, elections, capitalism, and more. According to Levin:

> America has turned from the most representative form of government to a de facto judicial tyranny. From same-sex marriage, illegal immigration, and economic socialism to partial-birth abortion, political speech, and terrorists' "rights," judges have abused their constitutional mandate by imposing their personal prejudices and beliefs on the rest of society. And we, the people, need not stand for it.[29]

In an excellent chapter on what the Supreme Court has done to damage religious freedom in America, Levin writes:

> The intensive and concerted effort to exclude references to religion or God from public places is an attack on our founding principles. It's an attempt to bolster a growing reliance on the government—especially the judiciary—as the source of our rights. But if our rights are not unalienable, if they don't come from a source higher than ourselves, then they're malleable at the will of the state. This is a prescription for tyranny.[30]

Mark Levin is absolutely correct. We, the people, need not stand for judicial tyranny any longer. That is why I have written this book, and it is why I joined with Rep. Todd Akin (R-MO) in promoting the passage of the Pledge Protection Act.

The Pledge Protection Act will help Americans take back their republican form of government from the robed masters who have usurped power from the executive and legislative branches of government—and from the American people!

The House of Representatives passed the Pledge Protection Act in 2006, but passage was blocked in the Senate by liberals of both parties who apparently prefer to have federal courts substitute their judgments for those of our legislators and for the will of the American people.

The Religious Freedom Coalition successfully helped drive this bill through the House with a vigorous petition campaign. Thousands of RFC supporters signed our Pledge Protection Act Petition and made their views known to members of the House on this important bill. Pressure must be brought to bear again on both the House and Senate to see the light—if they don't, they should feel the heat from angry constituents. This legislation isn't simply about the Pledge of Allegiance. It is about taking back control of our government from a tyrannical judicial oligarchy.

Federal judges—especially liberal activist judges—need to clearly understand they are only one branch of a government with three branches. They must be sent a message that we, the people, govern this nation and not unelected, arrogant judges like Stephen Reinhardt who seem to view themselves as superior to the rest of us. Reinhardt and his ilk—those who inhabit lifetime federal judgeships—need to have their power drastically cut back so self-government can be restored to our nation.

The fact is that today, we do not live in a self-governing democratic system. Why? Because every act of Congress and every law passed by state legislatures and every initiative passed by the American people—are all subject to the scrutiny of federal judges. These activist judges have usurped power from the executive and legislative branches, and operate more like Marxist or Fascist dictators than simply one branch of our government.

Judge Robert Bork, writing in his introduction to *Coercing Virtue*, has defined activist judges in these terms:

> Activist judges are those who decide cases in ways that have no plausible connection to the law they purport to be applying, or who stretch or even contradict the meaning of that law. They arrive at results by announcing principles that were never contemplated by those who wrote and voted for the law. The law in question is usually a constitution, perhaps because the language of a constitution tends to be general and, in any event, judicial overreaching is then virtually immune to correction by the legislature or by the public. . . . *It is often easier to predict the outcome of a case by knowing the names of the judges than by knowing the applicable legal doctrine* [emphasis added].[31]

Judge Bork's last sentence above is a key to understanding the battle we're facing over religious freedom in America. The opponents of religious freedom are not limited to Michael Newdow but include renegade federal judges who obviously have no respect for the Constitution, the other two branches of government, or the American people's right to govern themselves.

Judge Bork's warning is the same sounded by Thomas Jefferson in the nineteenth century over the unrestrained power of the federal courts to sit in judgment of all laws. It is important to be reminded once again of Jefferson's concern about federal courts:

> To consider the judges as the ultimate arbiters of all constitutional questions [is] a very dangerous doctrine indeed, and one which would place us under the despotism of an oligarchy. . . . The Constitution has erected no such single tribunal, knowing that to whatever hands confided, with the corruptions of time and party, its members would

become despots. It has more wisely made all the departments co-equal and co-sovereign within themselves.
(Thomas Jefferson to William C. Jarvis, 1820)[32]

In 1832, President Andrew Jackson stated the clear role of
the courts in relationship to the executive and legislative
branches of government. He observed:

> Each public officer who takes an oath to support the Con-
> stitution swears that he will support it as he understands
> it, and not as it is understood by others . . . The opinion of
> judges has no more authority over Congress than the
> opinion of Congress had over the judges, and on that point
> the President is independent of both. The authority of the
> Supreme Court must not, therefore, be permitted to con-
> trol the Congress or the Executive.[33]

In his first inaugural address in 1861, President Abraham
Lincoln expressed the same concern over federal courts and their
proper role. He said:

> . . . the candid citizen must confess that if the policy of the
> Government upon all vital questions affecting the whole
> people is to be irrevocably fixed by decisions of the
> Supreme Court the instant they are made in ordinary lit-
> igation between parties to personal actions, the people will
> have ceased to be their own rulers, having to that extent
> practically resigned their Government into the hands of
> that eminent tribunal.[34]

In short, Jefferson, Jackson, and Lincoln, along with Bork,
Levin, and others, have correctly diagnosed the dangers of an
out-of-control federal court system. As Lincoln said, to turn

over all decisions about law to the Supreme Court is to turn the entire government over to judges. This is tyranny, not democratic government.

Today, the "Living Constitution" ideology that has infected the minds of such men as Supreme Court Justice Stephen Breyer and Judge Stephen Reinhardt, must be defeated if we are ever to restore self-government to this nation.

As noted earlier, the House of Representatives twice had the courage to pass the Pledge Protection Act, but it then stalled in the Senate. We will explain the origins and purposes of this bill in the next chapter. Until we restrain the ability of federal courts to hear cases involving religious freedom and other moral concerns, we will continue to suffer at the hands of our robed masters.

With the appointment of Chief Justice John Roberts and Associate Justice Samuel Alito to the Supreme Court in 2005 and 2006, there is a chance the high court can be reformed from its liberal bent. There was still a social liberal majority on the Court that should be replaced for the good of the nation. This and future presidents must continue to nominate judicial conservatives to replace retiring judges on the entire federal bench. This will be a slow, laborious process and any president with social conservative leanings will be stonewalled by socially liberal Senators from both parties every step of the way.

Passage of legislation such as the Pledge Protection Act, however, can eventually solve many of the problems caused by liberal activist judges on the federal bench. They will simply be prohibited from ruling on such cases! I imagine this will cause them great consternation because their ability to engage in social engineering will be cut off. Perhaps this restriction on their ability to usurp power will encourage them to retire! Our nation would surely be better off if men like Stephen Reinhardt retired from the bench.

CHAPTER 8

Protecting the Pledge and Our Heritage of Rights

A S we've seen in previous chapters, the threat posed by anti-religious extremists like Michael Newdow to the Pledge of Allegiance and the phrase "under God" is merely a symptom of what has gone drastically wrong with our system of government. We no longer live in a democratic system where the legislatures and the people make the laws; we live in what amounts to a judicial tyranny run by unelected federal judges with lifetime appointments and immense power.

Judge Robert Bork's reference to Supreme Court justices as "our robed masters" could also as easily be applied to lower federal court judges such as those on the Ninth Circuit Court of Appeals in San Francisco.

Mark Levin, author of *Men in Black: How the Supreme Court Is Destroying America*, is even more blunt in his assessment of how the Supreme Court has undermined democratic government in America over the past decades.

Judicial activists are nothing short of radicals in robes— contemptuous of the rule of law; subverting the Constitution at will, and using their public trust to impose their policy preferences on society. In fact, no radical political movement has been more effective in undermining our system of government than the judiciary. And with each Supreme Court term, we hold our collective breath hoping the justices will do no further damage, knowing full well they will disappoint. Such is the nature of judicial tyranny.[1]

The system erected by federal judges is thoroughly undemocratic and violates the entire notion of self-government in a republic. This is not what the Founding Fathers had in mind when they created a system with three coequal branches of government, each with a clear separation of powers and functions. They designed this system to avoid the possibility our nation could ever be ruled by tyrannical kings. Yet, that is precisely what has happened. This change in the power of the federal judiciary is due largely to the inaction of Congress and the aggressiveness of these judges to seize whatever power they can.

We need to remember Thomas Jefferson's expressed concern over the trouble an out-of-control judiciary could cause our republic. Recall his prophetic words written to Edward Livingston in 1825:

> This member of the Government [the judiciary] was at first considered as the most harmless and helpless of all its organs. But it has proved that the power of declaring what the law is, *ad libitum* [at will], by sapping and mining slyly and without alarm the foundations of the Constitution, can do what open force would not dare attempt.[2]

Jefferson would undoubtedly agree with Mark Levin that the federal judiciary has operated as a subversive element within our government, undermining the right of the people to govern themselves.

The Ninth Circuit Court of Appeals, of course, is the most subversive of all the lower federal courts. Currently, we face the

ironic situation that the First Amendment to the Constitution—
which protects the free exercise of religion and free speech—is
being used by Ninth Circuit Court judges to censor free speech
and to violate the right of American children to acknowledge
that our nation was founded "under God." Only in an "Alice in
Wonderland" story or a George Orwell novel could *censorship of
speech* be considered protecting speech.

The War against Christianity

The battle over the words "under God" in the Pledge is only one
part of a larger war against Christianity and against free speech.
This battle is being waged not only in the United States but also
around the world.

In 1998, I was involved in the case of a New York City
sixth-grade teacher named Mildred Rosario. She was fired from
her job because she tried to comfort children in her class when
one of their classmates drowned. Her crime? She told the children that their classmate was in heaven. During the conversa-
tion, children asked her to explain what heaven was like. She
was fired by the board of education within a week.

I was outraged by the injustice against her and was contacted by Reverend Dr. Melvin Walker, who asked me to come
to New York to be part of a press conference on behalf of Mrs.
Rosario. A week after the press conference, Hispanic and black
pastors organized a demonstration in front of the board of
education building to protest Mrs. Rosario's unjust firing.
More than one thousand irate citizens demonstrated—and the
police brought out extra forces to quell any potential violence.
The fire department also showed up with high-pressure hoses
and an ambulance.

At the time, I vowed to continue fighting for Mrs. Rosario's
right to express her Christian faith in school and for her rein-
statement. Unfortunately, the board of education refused to

budge and Mrs. Rosario lost her job for expressing her faith to students and praying for them.

Mrs. Rosario's case gave renewed energy to my lobbying efforts in Congress to see passage of the Religious Freedom Amendment (RFA) to the Constitution. I had launched a petition campaign to get cosponsors for the RFA, but a vote in the House on June 4, 1998, fell short of the 290 votes needed for passage.

The RFA was a simple amendment. It read:

> To secure the people's right to acknowledge God according to the dictates of conscience:
> - The people retain the right to pray and to recognize their religious beliefs, heritage, and traditions on public property, including schools;
> - The United States and the States shall not establish any official religion nor require any person to join in prayer or religious activity.[3]

This amendment was sponsored by Rep. Ernest Istook (R-OK). In 2005, Rep. Istook refiled the RFA and immediately obtained over one hundred cosponsors for it. I launched another campaign to urge the supporters of the RFA to contact their legislators to have them add their names to the Religious Freedom Amendment.

In my petition urging passage of the Religious Freedom Amendment, I noted that "the Religious Freedom Amendment . . . echoes the standard that has been adopted and applied by each and every one of our fifty states, because each and every one of them has chosen to include an express reference to God within their State constitutions." I then listed the states and their references to God in their official documents. (This list is included as Appendix A at the end of this book.) Unfortunately Congressman Istook left Congress in 2006 to run for governor of Oklahoma and will no longer be available to fight this great cause in the Congress.

The Mildred Rosario case is only one of numerous religious freedom battles I've been involved in over the years. In 2000, I helped organize a rally at West Monroe High School in Louisiana, along with my friend Mat Staver of the Liberty Counsel. The high school had come under attack from the ACLU.

What was the ACLU's problem with Monroe High School? The incident that sparked ACLU anger involved several students who were badly injured in a car accident. The school principal had announced over the intercom that students should *pray* for the injured teenagers! The ACLU protested that this was a violation of the alleged separation of church and state.

As I said at the time, the people who run the ACLU are just plain nuts! They aren't for free speech. They demand the right to control what speech is acceptable and what isn't. In the ACLU view, pornography—even child pornography—is protected free speech, but public prayer isn't! The ACLU is currently representing the North American Man/Boy Love Association (NAMBLA) in a lawsuit. Most gay organizations distance themselves from the NAMBLA extremists—but the ACLU does not. The ACLU claims NAMBLA's Web site is protected speech—but they routinely file lawsuits to stifle the free speech of children who might want to pray. It's clear which side of free speech the ACLU is on. Free speech is available only for liberal or socially destructive causes, such as NAMBLA's promotion of sex with boys under the age of twelve.

The assault on Christianity is not only a problem in the United States. It is an international problem. In 1998 a Canadian Christian, Mark Harding, was convicted on a federal hate crime charge of distributing pamphlets about Islam outside a public high school in Toronto in 1997. Harding was protesting the school's policy of setting aside a prayer room for Muslims but banning Christianity, Hinduism, or Buddhism from the school.

Harding lost all his appeals in 2002 and was sentenced by a court to 340 hours of community service under the authority of the Islamic Society of North America (ISNA).

The general secretary of ISNA, Mohammad Ashraf, decided Harding was to be forced to learn about Islam. Harding said Ashraf told him if he said anything negative about Islam, Ashraf would make sure he was sent to jail for violating his community service agreement.

Ashraf made him read *Toward Understanding Islam* by Sayyid Abdul A'la Maududi. On page twelve of the book, it describes in these words a *kafir*—an infidel (someone who does not follow Islam): "Such a man . . . will spread confusion and disorder on the earth. He will without the least compunction, shed blood, violate other men's rights, be cruel to them, and create disorder and destruction in the world. His perverted thoughts and ambitions, his blurred vision and disturbed scale of values, and his evil-spelling activities would make life bitter for him and for all around him."

When interviewed by *WorldNetDaily*, Mark Harding said it was clear Ashraf "intended to make sure I understood that I was a kafir."[4]

Canada's hate crime law bars any statement that "willfully promotes hatred" against religious groups. In short, Mark Harding's free speech and religious freedom do not exist as long as he lives in Canada.

Imagine the uproar among liberals in Canada if a court had forced a Muslim to undergo Christian indoctrination and forbade him from saying negative things about Christianity.

Hate crime laws are also being used against Christians in other parts of the world. In late 2005, Swedish pastor Ake Green was acquitted of committing a "hate crime" against homosexuals because he preached a sermon from the Bible condemning homosexual conduct.[5] Sweden had added "sexual orientation" to its hate speech law in 2003—and Green was prosecuted for faithfully preaching God's Word from the pulpit.

Will the Bible become hate speech in the United States?

Will legislatures pass "hate crime" laws to criminalize sermons that may make non-Christians feel uncomfortable?

No assault on freedom of religion is too out-of-bounds for an ACLU lawyer—especially when he can currently collect huge court-ordered fees from a judgment or settlement.

Freedom of speech is also being stifled in Europe by nations that have passed "anti-defamation" laws against religious faiths. Most of the laws appear to be used against individuals who are critical of radical Islam.

Italian author Oriana Fallaci was ordered to stand trial for defaming Islam in her book *The Force of Reason.* In it she said Islam "sows hatred in the place of love and slavery in the place of freedom."[6] According to an Italian judge, she was guilty of violating Italy's anti-defamation law.

Censorship in the American Workplace

In the United States, political correctness has taken such root in businesses that free speech and the free exercise of religious belief are both being suppressed. As a result, a culture of fear is gripping many in the workplace.

For centuries the workplace has been free and open to ideas and cultures. The American workplace was the fire under the melting pot that made this nation great. No more! The workplace in America is no longer a melting pot; it's a multicultural nightmare in which workers live in a constant state of justifiable fear.

Major corporations now hire multicultural consulting firms to train managers to suppress the thoughts and the speech of employees. Break rooms once full of laughter and jokes are now often silent as they are monitored for politically correct content. Memos are posted on the walls reminding employees not to use "offensive" language. Two decades ago such a memo would mean not to curse or use the Lord's name in vain. Today "offensive" means uttering the words "Merry Christmas" or inviting someone to your church's Christmas pageant. In much of today's corporate culture, no one may say anything, write anything, or wear anything that might offend some minority, either real or perceived.

Just prior to Christmas in 2005, one of the suppliers of the Religious Freedom Coalition sent a newsletter along with the monthly statement. The newsletter contained a column entitled "Culturally Sensitive Celebrations." Some of the tips included:

- Be aware of the seasonal religious observances that may affect your workforce.
- Don't focus on Christmas, Hanukkah, and Kwanzaa. . . . Consider Ramadan or Diwali too.

Kwanzaa is not even a religious holiday, but rather a celebration of black culture invented by an American businessman just a few years ago. In addition Diwali and Ramadan celebrations have nothing to do with the month of December, but the multicultural consulting firm of Novations/J. Howard wanted its many corporate clients to mix all of these in with Christmas anyway.

The newsletter's featured tips from Novations also advised, "During the upcoming winter holidays, decorate with snowflakes or a winter theme, rather than the traditional red and green." Finally corporate officials were advised to move any parties or events to January, apparently so no one could confuse it with a Christmas party. The newsletter article stated this would be beneficial because it would stop, ". . . letting religious and cultural differences keep us apart." America's major corporations are leaders in creating a new right, the right "not to be offended."

This new right, which began in Scandinavian nations, has spread throughout Europe and Canada and now threatens free speech in the United States. As I noted earlier, in Sweden a pastor was sentenced to jail time for offending gays, and in Canada men have been fined and forced to work in mosques because they offended Muslims. In America those who utter the word "Christmas" are now targeted as offenders by the same people who champion the "hate crimes" laws that squelch free speech in Europe and Canada.

In the strange new politically correct world, even members of protected groups can find themselves in trouble for criticizing other protected groups. Consider this: Is a gay allowed to publicly criticize Islam, since homosexual acts are punishable by death in several Islamic countries?

The right to free speech is not compatible with this new so-called right not to be offended; the two "rights" are innately contradictory. In some nations, such as Canada, the right to free speech has been lost, and there is a question as to whether this book can be sold in that nation. Even Christian ministries in the United States must alter their TV and radio broadcasts to suit Canadian censors, and the written word is stopped at the Canadian border if it is deemed offensive to any group. But free speech is still salvageable in the United States. To salvage free speech, the politically correct corporate culture in America must be destroyed before it creeps into government and destroys our rights.

Defending the Pledge, Free Speech, And Freedom of Religion

As I have studied the history of our nation and the terrible distortions of the concept of "separation of church and state," I am convinced many of the threats to religious freedom and free speech can be squelched by passing the Pledge Protection Act. Why? Because it will restrict federal activist judges from issuing badly flawed rulings on matters that should more properly be dealt with by state courts and state legislatures.

The Pledge Protection Act is the brainchild of Rep. Todd Akin (R-MO), who is a student of America's Christian history and our Constitution. He saw the need for legislation to control activist federal judges as soon as he learned Michael Newdow's lawsuit was headed to the liberal Ninth Circuit Court. He began looking for legislative remedies to fix the problem of activist judges who disdain the Constitution, and, with the help of his colleagues on a House committee, he crafted the Pledge Protection Act.

I am reprinting the simple text of this legislation below and will let Rep. Todd Akin explain why this legislation is so desperately needed. Congressman Akin has been dedicated to this mission, having twice introduced the bill in the House and watched it pass, and now has introduced an updated version into the 110th Congress in 2007.

This is the text of the legislation as first introduced in the 108th Congress:

108th CONGRESS
2d Session
H. R. 2028
AN ACT

To amend title 28, United States Code, with respect to the jurisdiction of Federal courts over certain cases and controversies involving the Pledge of Allegiance.

HR 2028 EH
108th CONGRESS
2d Session
H. R. 2028
AN ACT

To amend title 28, United States Code, with respect to the jurisdiction of Federal courts over certain cases and controversies involving the Pledge of Allegiance.

*Be it enacted by the Senate and House of Representatives
of the United States of America in Congress assembled,*

SECTION 1. SHORT TITLE.
"This Act may be cited as the Pledge Protection Act of
2004."

SECTION 2. LIMITATION ON JURISDICTION.
(a) In General—Chapter 99 of title 28, United States
Code, is amended by adding at the end the following:
Sec. 1632. Limitation on jurisdiction
"No court created by Act of Congress shall have any jurisdiction, and the Supreme Court shall have no appellate
jurisdiction, to hear or decide any question pertaining to
the interpretation of, or the validity under the Constitution of, the Pledge of Allegiance, as defined in section 4
of title 4, or its recitation." The limitation in this section
shall not apply to the Superior Court of the District of
Columbia or the District of Columbia Court of Appeals.

(b) Clerical Amendment—The table of sections at the
beginning of chapter 99 of title 28, United States Code, is
amended by adding at the end the following new item:
"1632. Limitation on jurisdiction."

—Passed the House of Representatives
September 23, 2004.

The Pledge Protection Act of 2004 passed by a vote of 247–173
in the House, but then died for lack of action in the Senate.

It passed again in the House on July 19, 2006, by a 260–
167 vote. It failed once again in the Senate, defeated by liberals who apparently prefer that judges should rule over us rather
than that the American people should legislate what they desire
through their elected representatives.

Congressman Akin was interviewed by the *Kansas City Star* (April 6, 2006) about the Pledge Protection Act. He told the paper, "The words 'under God' are not just there for window dressing, but they address a central aspect of what America is all about: We believe there is a God, even though we don't agree on exactly what his name is. God grants basic rights to people and government's job is to protect those rights. That's why that phrase is in our pledge and is in need of defense."

The *Kansas City Star* also interviewed me. I told the reporter, "The courts don't interpret law anymore, they simply make law. . . . The Congress believed that an appropriate pledge to the flag would contain the words 'under God.' It was so vastly and overwhelmingly passed that the president (Dwight D. Eisenhower) immediately signed it into law. But now the courts say someone is offended. It's not a church-state issue. It's an issue of the federal courts granting a new right—the right not to be offended. This is intolerable in a free society."[7]

The Need for the Pledge Protection Act

What would the Pledge Protection Act accomplish? It would enable Congress to enforce its constitutionally mandated authority to restrict the kinds of cases that federal courts can hear. It would also restrict federal courts (including the Supreme Court) from ruling on State Supreme Court cases by limiting the courts' appellate jurisdiction.

This type of legislation would put severe restrictions on activist liberal judges—such as those on the Ninth Circuit in California—who routinely make up novel rulings in order to impose their own leftist ideologies upon millions of Americans. The "under God" ruling against the Pledge is a prime example of how renegade judges distort and misinterpret our laws and what church-state separation really means.

When the Pledge Protection Act of 2005 was being debated in Congress and in the media, it was amazing to see the flood of distortions coming from liberal members of Congress and from the various anti-Christian organizations opposed to the passage of this important bill. Here is just a sampling of the outrageous comments coming from anti-Christian zealots:

Rep. Jerold Nadler (D-NY): "We're playing with fire here, we are playing with the national unity of this country."[8]

Rep. John Conyers (D-MI): [The Pledge Protection Act is] "an unconstitutional and unnecessary court-stripping bill that would eliminate access to the federal judiciary for a specific group of claims. My Republican colleagues seem to have forgotten that it is the judicial branch that has often been the sole protector of the rights of minority groups against the will of the popular majority. Any proposal to interfere with this role by stripping the courts of their powers sets a dangerous precedent that would harm all Americans."[9]

Rev. Barry Lynn, executive director of Americans United for Separation of Church and State: "This bill [Pledge Protection Act] is a dramatic assault on the courts and individual rights, wrapped in phony patriotism. This is election-year grandstanding at its worst. The supporters of this bill have shown callous disregard for long-standing constitutional principles. The federal courts should be open to all Americans seeking protection of their constitutional rights. I am confident that the Senate will bury this bill, as it so richly deserves."[10]

One can only wonder how implementing Article 3, Section 2, of the Constitution can somehow be unconstitutional. Is

Rep. John Conyers claiming the Constitution itself is now unconstitutional and can't be used by Congress to control renegade federal judges? This kind of thinking from liberal legislators is
absurd—and clearly shows why we need to control liberal judges
and keep liberals from gaining majority status in Congress.

Rep. Todd Akin Defends the Pledge

Rep. Akin eloquently defended the Pledge Protection Act in
numerous media interviews—especially in 2004—when the Act
was being vigorously debated in the 108th Congress. Here are
a few of his important observations on the bill and why it must
be passed:

> The courts are the ones who initiated this entire discussion.
> The legislature is acting defensively to protect a long-stand-
> ing tradition. . . . [The Declaration of Independence is based
> upon the notion] that there is a Creator, that the Creator is
> the guarantor and source of basic human rights, and the
> job of civil government is to protect those rights. That is
> foundational to everything that America has been . . .[11]
>
> [It is wrong] if we allow activist judges to start creat-
> ing law and say that it is wrong to somehow allow school
> children to say "under God" in the Pledge. . . .[12]
>
> [Michael Newdow's lawsuit] is a disturbing effort to
> stifle the right of the children of our country to echo a com-
> mitment to what the Declaration calls "a firm reliance on
> Divine Providence," and must not be allowed to stand. . . .[13]
>
> The Supreme Court and courts in general have been
> usurping the role of the legislative branch of government.
> They've been legislating from the bench and they've been
> inventing various broad, sweeping powers or inventing
> policy that they find intuitively in the Constitution which
> to any clear-minded person is not there at all. . . .[14]

If we allow activist judges to say that it is wrong for school children to say "under God," we are emasculating the foundation of our country. Are they going to tell us to get rid of "In God We Trust" on our walls, that we can't have chaplains in the Congress? Are we going to get rid of the Gettysburg Address? How far should we let them go? . . .[15]

Rep. Akin's bill is supported by many constitutional scholars, including John Eidsmoe, Professor of Law at Thomas Goode Jones School of Law in Montgomery, Alabama. Professor Eidsmoe has observed:

I think Congressman Akin has a good bill and I think it is entirely in line with the Constitution. The Constitution clearly says that the Congress can limit the appellate jurisdiction of the Supreme Court. The framers wouldn't have put that check in the Constitution if they hadn't intended that [it] be used from time to time and it certainly isn't a check that is being used today. I think it is entirely appropriate in a circumstance like this.

Rep. Akin's Counsel Details
Legality of Pledge Protection Act

Brent Tantillo, who served as a legal counsel and legislative assistant to Rep. Akin during the 109th session of Congress, issued an important memo in March 2006 that goes into great detail describing the legality of the Pledge Protection Act.

Tantillo quoted Alexander Hamilton, who wrote in No. 80 of the *Federalist Papers* that Congress has "broad" authority to amend federal court jurisdiction "to remedy perceived abuse." According to Hamilton: ". . . it ought to be recollected that the national legislature will have ample authority to make such

exceptions, and to prescribe such regulations as will be calcu-
lated to obviate or remove these inconveniences."[16]

Hamilton also wrote that the Supreme Court and lower
federal courts have appellate jurisdiction to hear state cases, but
"shall be subject to such exceptions and regulations as the
national legislature may prescribe. This will enable the government to modify it in such a manner as will best answer the ends
of public justice and security."[17]

The Constitution and the Founding Fathers are clear: Congress has the rightful authority to limit the jurisdiction of the
Supreme Court and federal courts to hear certain cases. For liberals to claim the Pledge Protection Act or other acts of Congress
that are intended to limit court jurisdiction are "unconstitutional"
is absolutely false and politically motivated. What liberals fear
is that they are going to lose control of our federal court system
and thus lose the power to force liberal social programs down
our throats by judicial fiat. What we are attempting to do is
restore the federal court system to its rightful role in our three
branches of government. As Thomas Jefferson so wisely
observed about our government—to assert that the judiciary has
final authority over all laws is for democratic government to
commit suicide. If judges have total power over us, self-government has ceased to exist.

Other Legislative Solutions Needed

The House once again passed the Pledge Protection Act in the
109th, as we expected it would. Had it passed the Senate as well,
it would still have been challenged in court. Yet, the Congress has
full authority to restrict the jurisdiction of federal courts, so it is
unlikely any federal court could reasonably determine that the
Constitution itself is somehow unconstitutional. Of course, anything is possible with creative liberal judges who believe the Constitution is a "living document" subject to redefinition.

In 2006, I spent considerable time going from office to office in the House of Representatives to encourage members to cosponsor the Pledge Protection Act. I met with success in many cases, including getting a commitment from House Majority Whip Roy Blunt (R-MO) to support passage of the Pledge Protection Act. All who promised their help, including the Majority Whip, kept their word.

In addition, the Religious Freedom Action Coalition solicited petitions from citizens to send to their elected representatives in Congress urging them to cosponsor the Act and to help get it passed as quickly as possible. Signed petitions for all 535 members of the House and Senate were received. I am convinced this petition campaign played a great part in bringing victory in the 109th session of the House. But, the battle was lost in the Senate, where social liberals of both parties were determined to kill this legislation. Religious freedom advocates must now repeat their efforts in the 110th or for that matter even the 111th Congress to protect "under God" in the Pledge.

More Action Is Needed

However, there is much more to be done. The Pledge Protection Act is only one bill that should hve been passed in order to take back our courts from liberal activist judges. One of those was the unique legislation proposed in the 109th Congress by Indiana Republican John Hostettler who, unfortunately, did not return to the 110th. The Public Expression of Religion Act, sponsored by Hostettler, took aim at the American Civil Liberties Union and other anti-Christian legal groups who reap millions of dollars in court-ordered fees when they win church-state lawsuits. Currently, attacking public displays of religious symbols is a cash cow for the ACLU because they routinely file hundreds of lawsuits throughout the United States to violate the religious freedom of Christians.

The Public Expression of Religion Act would have amended
the Civil Rights Attorney's Fees Act of 1976 to prohibit groups
like the ACLU from being awarded attorney's fees in religious
establishment clause cases. The ACLU has been exploiting this
law for its own enrichment at the expense of American taxpayers,
who have been forced to pay fees to the ACLU when this anti-
Christian group files a lawsuit against a school district or a local
or state government. Under Hostettler's bill, the ACLU would
have to pay for the lawsuits it files. Since the main business of the
ACLU is blackmail resulting in outrageous settlements for legal
fees, the organization's finances would be greatly hurt.[18]

Even former ACLU attorney Rees Lloyd has spoken out
against the ACLU's tactics and fully supports Hostettler's legislation. According to Lloyd, the ACLU "has perverted, distorted, and exploited the Civil Rights Act . . . to turn it into a
lawyer enrichment act."

In a podcast aired by Hostettler in 2005, Lloyd said:

> Not only can the ACLU bring these lawsuits and compel
> taxpayers to pay them to destroy the public display of our
> American history and heritage, but so can Islamist terror-
> ists or Islamist sympathizers in our midst. All they have to
> do is walk into court, make their claim that they're
> offended by the sight of a cross or other religious symbol,
> and they're going to win the case because judges follow
> one another under *stare decisis* [previous court decisions].[19]

Lloyd told Hostettler he became disgusted with the ACLU
over the ACLU's lawsuit against a cross on a veteran's memorial
on public land in the Mojave Desert a few years ago. "For me, that
was the one step taken too far. Now, for the first time, the ACLU
was attacking the very veterans who secured their freedom."

In describing the need for the Public Expression of Religion
Act, Hostettler said the ACLU and other anti-Christian groups

have found a new civil liberty, a right to be protected " 'from religion,' which is found nowhere in the Constitution, nowhere in the Bill of Rights."

Hostettler says the ACLU routinely bullies local authorities—especially school authorities—when children pray at commencement ceremonies or write papers about Jesus Christ. An ACLU chapter can sue the school district and the district will often cave to avoid a costly legal battle. The ACLU then wins attorney's fees and uses that money to file more lawsuits attacking religious freedom. Hostettler pointed out that the ACLU lawsuit against Alabama Supreme Court Justice Roy Moore over the display of the Ten Commandments was settled quickly by the state in order to avoid paying outrageous attorney's fees that amounted to $500,000 before the lawsuit was settled. Rees Lloyd has correctly criticized what he calls the "terrorizing litigation tactics of the ACLU."

In addition to the Pledge Protection Act and the Public Expression of Religion Act, the 109th Congress also debated passage of the Constitution Restoration Act sponsored by Senator Richard Shelby (R-AL). The Constitution Restoration Act would prohibit federal judges (including the Supreme Court) from issuing rulings involving the acknowledgment of God "as the sovereign source of law, liberty, or government." It also would prohibit judges from using foreign court decisions in their rulings. Judges who violate the bans in this bill can be impeached. Former Supreme Court Justice Sandra Day O'Connor admitted that during her tenure she had considered European treaties, and even the unratified European Constitution, in reaching her decisions rather than our Constitution.

We Must Have Judicial Conservatives in Federal Courts

As we saw in chapter 7, renegade federal judges like the ones on the Ninth Circuit Court of Appeals in San Francisco have basically declared war on representative self-government in the United States. They rule as judicial tyrants and legislate from the bench believing in their foolishness that they have greater knowledge than the collective electorate. They impose their ideologies upon all of us—without restraint and apparently being void of conscience.

The battle for religious freedom and the preservation of free speech in America will not be won by legislation alone. It must also be won by lobbying for the confirmation of judicial conservatives to the federal bench. The vicious smears of Judge John Roberts and Judge Samuel Alito when they were nominated to serve on the Supreme Court are recent examples of the desperation of liberal special interest groups who fear the loss of their power over the judiciary.

Liberal groups like the ACLU, People for the American Way, Americans United for Separation of Church and State, the Freedom from Religion Foundation, and others understand that their outrageous social policies can seldom be implemented through state legislatures or through Congress. So, they depend upon liberal judges to impose social engineering upon us through judicial edicts that violate the will of the majority of the American people.

The predominantly liberal federal court system is the area of government that leftist ideologues can most easily use to force their ideas upon us in an undemocratic way. Liberals, for all their talk about how much they love the "people," are lying. They really don't believe in majority rule; they prefer totalitarian left-wing judges, who force us to participate in liberalism's favorite social engineering projects.

Fortunately, the American people are waking up to the tyrannical rule of judges—and they're beginning to lobby aggressively for the confirmation of judicial conservatives to the bench. The battle for judges centers in the Senate Judiciary Committee, where, for now, conservative senators are in the majority. Every judicial conservative nominated by a Republican president faces vilification, character assassination, and distortion of his or her judicial record. The attacks are nearly too much to bear for some nominees and many have dropped out of the running because of the attacks and delays in confirmation, engineered by the far-left senators on the Judiciary Committee.

Just after Justice Alito was sworn in, I was present at a reception honoring him at the White House. His wife, Martha Ann, recalled how she had been forced to leave the Senate hearing room crying because she could not bear to her the untruths being told about her husband by senators. That part was on TV. However, she also told me that she went to a window and saw dozens of young volunteers wearing bright red pro-Alito tee shirts. Seeing all those demonstrating in favor of her husband gave her the strength to return to the hearing room. Those shirts were designed and supplied by the Religious Freedom Action Coalition of which I am an officer.

The ideologues who mount such personal attacks to promote their agendas have included Senators Ted Kennedy, Chuck Schumer, Dick Durbin, Diane Feinstein, Joseph Biden, and others. Their shameful displays during the televised Alito and Roberts hearings should have alarmed Americans. Their consistent disregard for the truth, misrepresenting of the records of these fine men, is a national travesty. Their willingness to say anything to defeat a judicial conservative shows just how wide the cultural gap is between the warring judicial philosophies. One side relies on the truth; the other side has to resort to lies and character assassination to achieve its objectives.

I am encouraged that Americans are finally getting fed up with judicial tyranny. I believe the Ninth Circuit Court of Appeals decision against the Pledge of Allegiance may have been the wake-up call Americans needed to realize something has gone drastically wrong with our federal courts.

During the Alito and Roberts confirmation hearings, the Capitol Hill switchboard and congressional e-mail in-boxes were bombarded with messages from Americans who clearly wanted the Senate to confirm these articulate judicial conservatives to the Supreme Court.

But the work is far from over. Liberals on the Supreme Court still dominate by a 5–4 majority and far too many lower federal court systems are dominated by renegade, ideologically driven, "living Constitution" liberals.

If we fail to gain a majority of judicial conservatives on the Supreme Court, we could face another twenty years of liberal court rulings against religious freedom.

The situation could actually become far worse than it is now because several liberal justices on the Supreme Court are openly advocating for the use of foreign court decisions in their rulings. If this becomes a routine practice, our entire American way of life could be determined by the anti-American, extremist, liberal positions of foreign judges in the European Union, Canada, South America, Asia, or Africa. Is it possible the Court could even use Sharia law as a guide in their decisions?

Judge Robert Bork, writing in *Coercing Virtue: The Worldwide Rule of Judges*, notes:

> International law is not law but politics. For that reason, it is dangerous to give the name "law," which summons up respect, to political struggles that are essentially lawless. The problem is not merely the anti-Americanism that grips foreign elites and shapes law; it is also the American intellectual class, which is largely hostile to the United States and uses alleged international law to attack the morality of its own government and society. International law becomes one more weapon in the domestic culture war.[20]

Judge Bork rightly fears the complete loss of national sovereignty if our federal courts, including the Supreme Court, begin looking overseas to anti-American elitist judges for decisions that will impact how we live.

We can prevent this internationalization of our laws by passing legislation to restrict the power of our federal courts to cite foreign decisions—and we must work diligently to make certain that conservatives can maintain power in Washington long enough to replace activist judges with judicial conservatives.

Our wonderful Constitution and our republican form of government are far too important to religious freedom and to the rest of the world, to let them fall again into the hands of liberals.

Are We Heading into Darkness or into the Light?

That depends upon you and me and what we are willing to do to fight for our freedoms. As our American soldiers have learned over the past 200-plus years of our history—freedom is costly. Hundreds of thousands of Americans have died to preserve our republic and more are dying each day in our nation's war against Islamic terrorism.

The battles we are fighting for religious freedom are today fought with e-mails, phone calls, letter-writing campaigns, and petitions. At this point in our history, the cost is one of time, not blood. However, if liberals succeed in maintaining their stranglehold on our federal courts, we could enter a time of darkness that may extinguish religious freedom under the guise of protecting the "right" of people not to be offended.

We do not have to fight an actual war to regain our freedoms from federal judges. Fortunately, we have the Internet, e-mail, telephones, and other ways of influencing our elected representatives to rid our nation of judicial tyranny. We must wage an educational war in order to regain freedoms lost—and to protect further encroachments by liberal judges upon religious freedom.

In closing, I am reminded again of the story of John Peter Muhlenberg, a pastor who was elected to the Virginia House of

Burgesses in 1774. He realized his country was asking more of him than he had given in the past—and he took action. I believe the same thing can be said of Americans who have been reluctant to actively participate in the political process by lobbying their legislators on behalf of religious freedom. It is time for us to take up the educational weapons at our disposal—letter-writing, petitioning, phone-calling, and the use of the Internet—to defend our Christian history and our legacy of religious freedom.

As I mentioned in chapter 2, Pastor Muhlenberg in 1775 preached a message from Ecclesiastes 3:1: "For everything there is a season, and a time for every purpose under heaven." He closed his sermon by saying, "In the language of the Holy Writ, there is a time for all things. There is a time to preach and a time to fight."

He then threw off his robes to reveal the uniform of a soldier in the Revolutionary Army. That afternoon, he led three hundred men off to join General George Washington's troops and became a colonel in the 8th Virginia Regiment. It was not an easy road he was taking, because he was to fight beside Washington in many difficult battles and endure the terrible winter at Valley Forge.

But Pastor Muhlenberg knew his time to preach was over and his time to fight for freedom had arrived.

Will we do the same in the twenty-first century by using the nonviolent weapons of education and lobbying to defend religious liberty?

Religious Expression in State Preambles, Mottos, Seals, and Flags

Alabama
"invoking the favor and guidance of Almighty God"

Alaska
"grateful to God and to those who founded our nation . . . in order to secure and transmit succeeding generations our heritage of political, civil, and religious liberty"

Arizona
"grateful to Almighty God for our liberties"

Arkansas
"grateful to Almighty God for the privilege of choosing our own form of government, for our civil and religious liberty"

California
"grateful to Almighty God for our freedom"

Colorado
"with profound reverence for the Supreme Ruler of the Universe"

Connecticut
"acknowledge with gratitude, the good providence of God"

Delaware	"Through Divine goodness, all men have by nature the rights of worshipping and serving their Creator according to the dictates of their own conscience."
Florida	"being grateful to Almighty God for our constitutional liberty"
Georgia	"relying upon the protections and guidance of Almighty God"
Hawaii	"grateful for Divine Guidance"
Idaho	"grateful to Almighty God for our freedom"
Illinois	"grateful to Almighty God for the civil, political and religious liberty which He has permitted us to enjoy and seeking His blessing upon our endeavors"
Indiana	"grateful to Almighty God for the free exercise of the right to choose our own Government"
Iowa	"grateful to the Supreme Being for the blessings hitherto enjoyed, and feeling our dependence on Him for a continuation of those blessings"
Kansas	"grateful to Almighty God for our civic and religious privileges"
Kentucky	"grateful to Almighty God for the civil, political, and religious liberties we enjoy"
Louisiana	"grateful to Almighty God for the civil, political, economic, and religious liberties we enjoy"

Maine	"acknowledging with grateful hearts the goodness of the Sovereign Ruler of the universe in affording us an opportunity, so favorable to the design; and imploring God's aid and direction in its accomplishments, do agree"
Maryland	"Scuto bonae voluntatis tuae coronasti nos" (5th Psalm, 12th verse: "With favor wilt thou compass us as with a shield")
Massachusetts	"acknowledging with grateful hearts, the goodness of the great Legislator of the Universe, in affording us, in the course of His providence, and opportunity"
Michigan	"grateful to Almighty God for the blessings of freedom"
Minnesota	"grateful to God for our civil and religious liberty"
Mississippi	"grateful to Almighty God, and invoking blessings of freedom"
Missouri	"with profound reverence for the Supreme Ruler of the Universe, and grateful for His goodness"
Montana	"grateful to Almighty God for the blessings of liberty"
Nebraska	"grateful to Almighty God for our freedom"
Nevada	"Grateful to Almighty God for our freedom in order to secure its blessings"

New Hampshire	"unalienable right to worship God according to the dictates of conscience" (from state constitution)
New Jersey	"grateful to Almighty God for the civil and religious liberty which He hath so long permitted us to enjoy, and looking to Him for a blessing upon our endeavors to secure . . ."
New Mexico	"grateful to Almighty God for the blessings of liberty"
New York	"grateful to Almighty God for our Freedom"
North Carolina	"grateful to Almighty God, the Sovereign Ruler of Nations"
North Dakota	"grateful to Almighty God for the blessings of civil and religious liberty"
Ohio	"grateful to Almighty God for our freedom"
Oklahoma	"Invoking the guidance of Almighty God"
Oregon	"to worship Almighty God" (from state constitution)
Pennsylvania	"grateful to Almighty God for the blessings of civil and religious liberty, and humbly invoking His guidance"
Rhode Island	"grateful to Almighty God for the civil and religious liberty which He hath so long permitted us to enjoy, and looking to Him for a blessing upon our endeavors"

South Carolina	"grateful to God for our liberties"
South Dakota	"grateful to Almighty God for our civil and religious liberties"
Texas	"Humbly invoking the blessings of Almighty God"
Tennessee	"to worship Almighty God" (from state constitution)
Utah	"Grateful to Almighty God for life and liberty"
Washington	"grateful to the Supreme Ruler of the Universe for our liberties"
West Virginia	"Since through Divine Providence we enjoy the blessings of civil, political and religious liberty . . . reaffirm our faith in and constant reliance upon God . . ."
Wisconsin	"grateful to Almighty God for our freedom"
Wyoming	"grateful to God for our civil, political, and religious liberties"
Vermont	"to worship Almighty God" (from state constitution)
Virginia	". . . duty which we owe to our Creator . . . mutual duty of all to practice Christian forbearance, love, and charity" (from state constitution)

Below is the current language of the Pledge Protection Act as offered by Congressman Todd Akin in the 110th Congress.

....

110th CONGRESS
1st Session
H. R. 699
To amend title 28, United States Code, with respect to the jurisdiction of Federal courts over certain cases and controversies involving the Pledge of Allegiance.

IN THE HOUSE OF REPRESENTATIVES
January 29, 2007

Mr. AKIN (for himself, Mr. FRANKS of Arizona, Mr. GINGREY, Mr. RAMSTAD, Mr. COLE of Oklahoma, Mrs. JO ANN DAVIS of Virginia, Mr. BURTON of Indiana, Mr. MILLER of Florida, Mr. MCKEON, Mr. NORWOOD, Mr. MCCOTTER, Mr. SENSENBRENNER, Mr. FOSSELLA, Mr. TOM DAVIS of Virginia, Mr. GOODE, Mr. HENSARLING, Mrs. MYRICK, Ms. GINNY BROWN-WAITE of Florida, Mr. MCHUGH, Mr. TIAHRT, Mr. RADANOVICH, Mr. PITTS, Mr. JORDAN of Ohio, Mr. PENCE, Mr. BURGESS, Mr. REYNOLDS, Mr. DAVID DAVIS of Tennessee, Mr. MARIO DIAZ-BALART of Florida, Mr. HERGER, Mr. GARY G. MILLER of California, Mr. GERLACH, Mr. LAMBORN, Mr. GARRETT of New Jersey, Mr. CHABOT, Mr. BOOZMAN, Mr. SALI, Mr. BAKER, Mr.

WILSON of South Carolina, Mrs. BLACKBURN, Mr. BACHUS, Mr. STEARNS, Mrs. CAPITO, Mr. BARTON of Texas, Mr. SAXTON, Mr. WELDON of Florida, Mr. RENZI, Mr. HUNTER, Mr. ROGERS of Michigan, Mrs. DRAKE, Mr. PEARCE, Mr. LATHAM, Mr. DAVIS of Kentucky, Mr. JONES of North Carolina, Mr. KINGSTON, Mr. FORTU-NAEO, Mr. WAMP, Mrs. EMERSON, and Mr. BISHOP of Georgia) introduced the following bill; which was referred to the Committee on the Judiciary

A BILL

To amend title 28, United States Code, with respect to the jurisdiction of Federal courts over certain cases and controversies involving the Pledge of Allegiance.

Be it enacted by the Senate and House of Representatives of the United States of America in Congress assembled,

SEC. 1. SHORT TITLE

This Act may be cited as the "Pledge Protection Act of 2007."

SEC. 2. LIMITATION ON JURISDICTION.

(a) In General—Chapter 99 of title 28, United States Code, is amended by adding at the end the following:

Sec. 1632. Limitation on jurisdiction

(a) Except as provided in subsection (b), no court created by Act of Congress shall have any jurisdiction, and the Supreme Court shall have no appellate jurisdiction, to hear or decide any question pertaining to the interpretation of, or the validity under the Constitution of, the Pledge of Allegiance, as defined in section 4 of title 4, or its recitation.

(b) The limitation in subsection (a) does not apply to—

(1) any court established by Congress under its power to make needful rules and regulations respecting the territory of the United States; or

(2) the Superior Court of the District of Columbia or the District of Columbia Court of Appeals.

(b) Clerical Amendment—The table of sections at the beginning of chapter 99 of title 28, United States Code, is amended by adding at the end the following new item:

1632. Limitation on jurisdiction.

SEC. 3. EFFECTIVE DATE.

This Act and the amendments made by this Act take effect on the date of the enactment of this Act and apply to any case that—

(1) is pending on such date of enactment; or

(2) is commenced on or after such date of enactment.

■ Endnotes

Chapter 1

1. Ron Collins, "A Brief History of the Pilgrims," Through the Looking Glass, Mayflowerfamilies.com/colonial_life/pilgrims.htm.

2. Joseph Gaer and Ben Siegel, *The Puritan Heritage: America's Roots in the Bible* (New York: New American Library, 1964), 19.

3. Ibid., 20.

4. Ibid., 21.

5. Ibid., 37.

6. Thomas Armitage, *A History of the Baptists*, "Banishment of Roger Williams," Fundamental Baptist Institute, fbinstitute.com/armitage/ch02.html.

7. Donzella Cross Boyle, *Quest of a Hemisphere* (Boston: Western Islands, 1970), 65.

8. Maryland Constitution, art. 36, http://www.msa.md.gov/msa/mdmanual/43const/html/00dec.html.

9. "Charter of Privileges Granted by William Penn, esq., to the Inhabitants of Pennsylvania and Territories, October 28, 1701," The Avalon Project at Yale Law School, http://www.yale.edu/lawweb/avalon/states/pa07.htm.

10. Benjamin J. Hart, *Faith and Freedom: The Christian Roots of American Liberty*, Leadership University, http://www.leaderu.com/orgs/cdf/ff/.

11. Ibid.

12. Ibid.

13. Ibid.

14. "The First Charter of Virginia; April 10, 1606," The Avalon Project of

Yale Law School, http://www.yale.edu/lawweb/avalon/states/va01.htm.

15. Charles E. Rice, "Gifts from God," *The New American,* May 3, 1993, http://www.jbs.org/node/1240.

16. Thomas Jefferson, "The Virginia Act for Establishing Religious Freedom," The Religious Freedom Page, University of Virginia, http://religiousfreedom.lib.virginia.edu/intro.html.

17. Thomas Jefferson, "The Declaration of Independence," National Archives, http://www.archives.gov/national-archives-experience/charters/declaration.html.

18. Constitution of the United States, National Archives, http://www.archives.gov/national-archives-experience/charters/constitution.html.

19. James H. Hutson, *Religion and the Founding of the American Republic* (Washington, DC: Library of Congress, 1998), 49.

20. Ibid., 84.

21. "Charles Carroll," Faith of Our Fathers, http://www.faithofourfathers.net/carroll.html.

22. Dave Miller, PhD, "America and Atheistic Evolutionists," Apologetics Press: Reason & Revelation, January 2007, http://www.apologetics-press.org/articles/3204.

23. "Dr. Benjamin Rush (1745–1813)," Faith of Our Fathers, http://www.faithofourfathers.org/biographies/rush.html.

24. David Barton, "Importance of Morality and Religion in Government," WallBuilders, http://www.wallbuilders.com/resources/search/detail.php?ResourceID=21.

25. "James Madison," Faith of Our Fathers, http://www.faithofourfathers.net/madison.html.

26. William Federer, *The Ten Commandments & Their Influence on American Law* (Amerisearch Inc., 2003), 141.

27. Clarence Manion, *The Key to Peace* (Chicago: The Heritage Foundation, 1951), 109–15.

28. Daniel Dreisbach, review of *The United States: A Christian Nation,* reprint ed., by David J. Brewer, *Journal of Church and State,* June 1997, http://findarticles.com/p/articles/mi_hb3244/is_199706/ai_n7941007.

29. Ibid.

30. B. F. Morris, *The Christian Life and Character of the Civil Institutions* (n.p.: Rickey & Carroll, 1864), Google Online Books, 249, http://books.google.com/books?vid=OCLC67250770&id=H92keUU_Xy8C&pg=RA1-PA11&lpg=RA1-PA11&dq=Christian+life+character+institutions+morris#PRA1-PA249,M1.

Chapter 2

1. Lester J. Cappon, ed., *The Adams-Jefferson Letters: The Complete Correspondence Between Thomas Jefferson and Abigail and John Adams* (Chapel Hill: University of North Carolina Press, 1998), Google Online Books, 550, http://books .google.com/books?vid=ISBN0807842303&id=SzSWYPOz6M8C&pg =PP1&lpg=PP1&ots=kTA0JDlQn&dq=adams+jefferson+letters+cappon&sig =6Uu2mBgm_GgUzTBA74TbUlV12OY (subscription required).

2. Gaer and Siegel, 70–71.

3. William Blackstone, "Selections from *Blackstone's Commentaries on the Laws of England,* Vol. 1, 1735," Amber Golding & Hofstetter, http:// www.agh-attorneys.com/4_william_blackstone.htm.

4. Chris Baker, "Algernon Sidney: Forgotten Founding Father," *The Freeman* 47, no. 10 (October 1997), http://www.fee.org/publications/the-freeman/ article.asp?aid=4822.

5. Ibid.

6. The Quotations Page, http://www.quotationspage.com/quote/3551.html.

7. John Locke, "Second Treatise on Government," http://www.constitution .org/jl/2ndtreat.htm.

8. Thomas Jefferson, "Declaration of Independence."

9. David Barton, "John Locke: Deist or Theologian," WallBuilders, http://www.wallbuilders.com/resources/search/detail.php?ResourceID=124.

10. C. Edward Merriam, *A History of American Political Theories,* U.S. Political Resources, http://political-resources.com/misc/art1sec8.htm.

11. Kim Ian Parker, *The Biblical Politics of John Locke* (Waterloo, ON: Wilfrid Laurier University Press, 2004), 35.

12. Francis Schaeffer, *A Christian Manifesto* (Westchester, IL: Crossway Books, 1982), 99.

13. Ibid., 105.

14. Richard P. Gildrie, *The Profane, the Civil, & the Godly: The Reformation of Manners in Orthodox New England, 1679–1749* (University Park: Penn State University Press, 1994), 85.

15. Ibid., 87.

16. Dan Oren, "Stamp of Approval," *Yale Alumni Magazine* (March 2001), http://www.yalealumnimagazine.com/issues/01_03/seal.html.

17. John F. Emling, *Value Perspectives Today: Toward an Integration With Jean Piaget's New Discipline in Relation to Modern Educational Leaders* (Fairleigh Dickinson University Press, 1997), Google Online Books, 68, http://

books.google.com/books?vid=ISBN0838619053&id=di1zm89jCZsC&pg
=PP1&lpg=PP1&ots=DVt4U7ngBo&dq=Value+Perspectives+Today:+Toward
+an+Integration+With+Jean+Piaget%27s+New+Discipline+in+Relation+to
+Modern+Educational+Leaders&sig=YhwxrSE3rMydBPfcn8bGGMTpRog.

18. Ibid.

19. "The New England Primer," Eastern Illinois University, http://www
.ux1.eiu.edu/~cfrnb/neprimer.html.

20. "The New England Primer 1777," Internet Sacred Text Archive,
http://www.sacred-texts.com/chr/nep/1777/index.htm.

21. John Winthrop, "On Liberty," The Constitution Society, www
.constitution.org/bcp/winthlib.htm.

22. William Penn, "Frame of Government of Pennsylvania," The Constitution Society, http://www.constitution.org/bcp/frampenn.htm.

23. Gaer and Siegel, 71.

24. Hutson, 42.

25. Ralph Waldo Emerson, "Concord Hymn," National Park Service,
http://www.nps.gov/archive/mima/hymn.htm.

26. Samuel Langdon, "Government corrupted by Vice, and recovered by
Righteousness" (reprinted in Thornton, *The Pulpit of the American Revolution*,
Boston, 1860, 233–58), Gospel Plow, http://users.frii.com/gosplow/langdon
.html.

27. Jonathan Mayhew, "A Discourse Concerning Unlimited Government
and Non-Resistance to the Higher Powers (Boston, 1750)," Lexrex, http://
www.lexrex.com/informed/otherdocuments/sermons/mayhew.htm.

28. David B. Kopel, "The Religious Roots of the American Revolution and
the Right to Keep and Bear Arms," http://www.davekopel.com/Religion/
Religious-Roots-of-the-American-Revolution.pdf.

29. "Give Me Liberty or Give Me Death," America's Christian History,
http://www.americanchristianhistory.com/christianhistory10.html.

Chapter 3

1. "Haymarket Square Riot," U-S-History.com, http://www.u-s-history
.com/pages/h750.html.

2. Eric Foner and John A. Garraty, eds., "Homestead Strike," *The Reader's
Companion to American History* (HoughtonMifflin, American Society of
American Historians, 1991).

3. L. Edward Purcell, *Immigration (Social Issues in American History Series)*
(Phoenix: Oryx Press, 1994), High Beam Research online database.

4. "Growth of the Knights of Columbus," Knights of Columbus, http://www.kofc.org/un/about/history/index.cfm.

5. Dr. John W. Baer, "The Life And Ideas of Francis Bellamy," *The Pledge of Allegiance: A Centennial History, 1892–1992* (Annapolis, MD: John W. Baer, 1992), http://history.vineyard.net/pdgech4.htm.

6. "Francis Bellamy," BookRags.com, http://www.bookrags.com/wiki/Francis_Bellamy.

7. "The Pledge of Allegiance: A Short History," ProBush.com, http://www.probush.com/pledge_of_allegiance_history.htm.

8. William Norman Grigg, "One Nation under the State?" *New American* (July 29, 2002), http://www.jbs.org/node/1141.

9. Scot M. Guenter, *The American Flag, 1777–1924: Cultural Shifts from Creation to Codification* (Madison, NJ: Fairleigh Dickinson University Press, 1990), 131.

10. *Congressional Record* (June 7, 1954).

11. Guenter, 132.

12. "Leon Czolgosz," *The American Experience*, PBS, http://www.pbs.org/wgbh/amex/1900/peopleevents/pande16.html.

13. "The Murder of Former Idaho Governor Frank Steunenberg," Digital History, http://www.digitalhistory.uh.edu/database/article_display.cfm?HHID=232.

14. Winston Churchill, "Iron Curtain Speech," National Center for Public Policy Research, http://www.nationalcenter.org/ChurchillIronCurtain.html.

15. Larry Witham, "'Under God' under Assault," *Insight on the News* (July 29, 2002), 32.

16. Tom Gibb, "Minister Reprises 'Under God' Sermon," *Pittsburgh Post-Gazette* (August 19, 2002), http://www.post-gazette.com/nation/20020819pledge0819p1.asp.

Chapter 4

1. Charles Russo, "The Pledge of Allegiance: Patriotic Duty or Unconstitutional Establishment of Religion?" *School Business Affairs* (July/August 2003), 27.

2. *Leoles v. Landers*, 302 U.S. 656 (1937).

3. *Gabrielli v. Knickerbocker*, 12 Cal.2d 85 (1938).

4. *Nicholls v. Mayor of Lynn*, 7 N.E.2d 577, 579 (Mass. 1937).

5. *Minersville School District v. Gobitis* (1940).

6. *Minersville School District v. Gobitis*, 310 U.S. 586 (1940).

7. Ibid.

8. Ibid.

9. Chuck Smith, "The Persecution of West Virginia Jehovah's Witnesses and the expansion of legal protection for religious liberty," *Journal of Church and State* (June 2001), http://findarticles.com/p/articles/mi_hb3244/is_200106/ai_n7953771.

10. *West Virginia State Board of Education v. Barnette*, 319 U.S. 624 (1943).

11. Ibid.

12. *Holden v. Elizabeth Board of Education*, 46 N.J. 281 (1966).

13. *Congressional Record*, February 8, 1954.

14. Congressman Oliver P. Bolton, *Congressional Record*, February 18, 1954.

15. Senator Kenneth Keating, *Congressional Record*, June 7, 1954.

16. Dahl research paper, "I Pledge Allegiance to What?: The History and Controversy over America's Pledge of Allegiance," James Madison University, http://www.jmu.edu/writeon/documents/2006/Dahl.pdf.

17. *State v. Lundquist*, 278 A.2d 263 (Md. 1971).

18. Lee Canipe, "Under God and anti-communist: how the Pledge of Allegiance got religion in Cold-War America," *Journal of Church and State* (March 2003), http://findarticles.com/p/articles/mi_hb3244/is_200303/ai_n7953567.

19. "Marbury v. Madison (1803)," Landmark Supreme Court Cases, Street Law & The Supreme Court Historical Society, http://www.landmarkcases.org/marbury/jefferson.html.

20. Ibid., http://www.landmarkcases.org/marbury/pdf/marbury_v_madison.pdf.

Chapter 5

1. Winston Churchill, "Iron Curtain Speech (Sinews of Peace)," The History Guide, http://www.historyguide.org/europe/churchill.html.

2. Whittaker Chambers, *Witness* (New York: Henry Regnery Company, 1952), 16–17.

3. W. Cleon Skousen, *The Naked Communist* (Salt Lake City: The Ensign Publishing Co., 1962), 307.

4. Ibid., 306.

5. Ibid., 3.

6. R. J. Rummel, *Death by Government* (New Brunswick, NJ: Transaction Publishers, 1994), University of Hawaii, http://www.hawaii.edu/powerkills/note1.htm.

7. Ibid.

8. Ibid.

9. Nada Mourtada-Sabbah, "Adopting 'In God We Trust' as the U.S. national motto," *Journal of Church and State* (September 2002), http://findarticles .com/p/articles/mi_hb3244/is_200209/ai_n7953651.

10. Ibid.

11. Ibid.

12. Ibid.

13. Ibid.

14. Ibid.

15. Ibid.

16. Ibid.

17. Ibid.

18. Ibid.

19. Ibid.

20. Ibid.

21. Ibid.

22. Ibid.

23. Ibid.

24. Ibid.

25. *Aronow v. United States*, 432 F.2d 242 (9th Cir. 1970).

26. Dwight D. Eisenhower, "Remarks Recorded for the 'Back-to-God' Program of the American Legion, February 20, 1955," The American Presidency Project, http://www.presidency.ucsb.edu/ws/index.php?pid=10414.

27. Pew Forum, "Brief on Merits" of Pledge of Allegiance, 11, http:// pewforum.org/religion-schools/pledge/docs/BriefonMerits.pdf.

28. Miller, "America and Atheistic Evolutionists.

29. John Quincy Adams, *Letters of John Quincy Adams, to His Son, on the Bible and its Teachings* (Auburn: James M. Alden, 1850), 61.

Chapter 6

1. Joshua Partlow, "Standing Up for the Right to Sit Down," *Washington Post* (December 1, 2005), B03.

2. *Everson v. Board of Education of the Township of Ewing et al.*, 330 U.S. 1 (1947), http://www.law.umkc.edu/faculty/projects/ftrials/conlaw/everson.html.

3. Ibid.

4. Ibid.

5. M. Stanton Evans, "What wall?—church and state," *National Review* (Jan. 23, 1995), http://www.findarticles.com/p/articles/mi_m1282/is_n1_v47/ai_16391209.

6. Ibid.

7. Hutson, 62.

8. Ibid.

9. Joseph A. P. De Feo, review of *Thomas Jefferson and the Wall of Separation between Church and State* by Daniel L. Dreisbach, *Catalyst* (March 2003), http://www.catholicleague.org/research/dreisbach.htm,.

10. Judge Robert Bork, "Separation of Church and State," *First Things* (December 2002), 43–47.

11. Judge Robert Bork, "Getting over the Wall," review of *Separation of Church and State* by Philip Hamburger, *American Enterprise Institute for Public Policy Research* (October 1, 2002), http://www.aei.org/publications/pubID.14251,filter .all/pub_detail.asp.

12. "Rehnquist's Dissent in *Wallace v. Jaffree* (1985)," The Belcher Foundation, http://www.belcherfoundation.org/wallace_v_jaffree_dissent.htm.

13. Madalyn Murray O'Hair, "The Battle is Joined," *American Atheist* 33, no. 3, http://www.atheists.org/courthouse/joined.html#battle.

14. William J. Murray, *Let Us Pray,* (New York: William Morrow & Company, 1995), 33.

15. Personal correspondence from Senator Santorum to the author.

16. Franky Schaeffer, *A Time for Anger: The Myth of Neutrality,* (Wheaton, IL: Good News/Crossway, 1982).

17. Marvin Olasky and John Perry, *Monkey Business* (Nashville: Broadman & Holman, 2005).

18. "In God We Trust on our currency," *The Forerunner* (November 1988), http://forerunner.com/forerunner/X0316_In_God_We_TrustCurre.html.

19. Valerie Richardson, "L.A. group demands cross back on county's seal," *Washington Times* (November 15, 2004, http://www.washtimes.com/national/20041115-122215-2330r.htm.

20. ACLU, "The Fish Must Go," July 9, 1999, http://www.aclu.org/religion/gen/16114prs19990709.html.

21. McCreary County v. American Civil Liberties Union of KY (03-1693) 354 F.3d 438, http://straylight.law.cornell.edu/supct/html/03-1693.ZS.html.

22. Sylvia Moreno, "Supreme Court on a Shoestring," *Washington Post* (February 21, 2005), A01.

23. Stephen B. Presser, "The Ten Commandments Mish-Mosh," *The American Spectator* October 2005), Northwestern University Law School, http://www.law.northwestern.edu/news/article_full.cfm?eventid=2164.

24. *Van Orden v. Perry* (03-1500), 351 F. 3d. 173, http://straylight.law.cornell.edu/supct/html/03-1500.ZS.html.

25. Presser, "The Ten Commandments Mish-Mosh."

26. Jordan Lorence, "Supremes: Shut down 'offended observers,'" WorldNet-Daily, February 26, 2005, http://www.wnd.com/news/ article.asp?ARTICLE_ID=43050.

27. Ibid.

28. *Stephen J. Williams v. Patricia Vidmar et al.*, Alliance Defense Fund, http://www.alliancedefensefund.org/userdocs/WilliamsvCupertinoComplaint.pdf.

29. Troy Anderson, "LA's Name Too Divine? 'Angels' Reference May Mean Trouble," *Los Angeles Daily News* (June 13, 2004), http://www.highbeam.com/doc/1G1-118158934.html.

30. Jodie Gilmore, "For Heaven's Sake, Don't Mention God," *New American* (January 10, 2005), http://www.questia.com/PM.qst?a=o&d=5008399939.

Chapter 7

1. Rob Boston, "One Nation Indivisible? 'Under God' Case at Supreme Court Tests Nation's Commitment to Church-State Separation, Religious Pluralism," *Church & State* 56, no. 11 (December 2003), 6, http://www.au.org/site/News2?JServSessionIdr002=kx4d3h8g23.app5b&abbr=cs_&page=NewsArticle&id=5294&security=1001&news_iv_ctrl=1093.

2. Michael Newdow, "Why I Did It: The 'Under God' And Chaplaincy Plaintiff Speaks Out," *Free Inquiry* 23, no. 1 (Winter 2002), http://www.secularhumanism.org/library/fi/newdow_23_1.html.

3. Ibid.

4. *Elk Grove Unified School District and David W. Gordon, Superintendent, v. Michael A. Newdow et al., Respondents,"* American Center for Law and Justice Amicus Brief, 2.

5. Rob Boston, "'Under God' at the High Court: Pledge Plaintiff Newdow Argues Well, but the Justices Seem Unreceptive" *Church & State* 57, no. 5 (May 2004), 4ff.

6. Ibid.

7. Ibid.

8. "Thomas Jefferson on Politics & Government," University of Virginia, http://etext.virginia.edu/jefferson/quotations/jeff0100.htm.

9. Ibid.

10. ACLJ Brief. (See Footnote 3.)

11. Ibid.

12. Ibid.

13. *Elk Grove Unified School District et al. v. Michael A. Newdow et al., Respondents,* Brief Amicus Curiae of the Knights of Columbus, December 19, 2003, 4.

14. *Elk Grove Unified School District v. Newdow.* http://a257.g.akamaitech .net/7/257/2422/14june20041230/www.supremecourtus.gov/opinions/03pdf/ 02-1624.pdf.

15. *Elk Grove Unified School District and David W. Gordon, Superintendent v. Michael A. Newdow,* Brief Amicus Curiae of American Atheists, http://www .atheists.org/courthouse/PledgeBrief.pdf.

16. Julia Duin, " 'Under God' Remains in Pledge; Court Reverses Ruling on Technicality," *Washington Times* (June 15, 2004), A01.

17. *Elk Grove Unified School District et al. v. Newdow et al.,* O'Connor concurring decision, http://caselaw.lp.findlaw.com/scripts/getcase.pl?court =US&vol=000&invol=02-1624#concurrence1.

18. Jon Ward, "Newdow Targets Use of Clergy," *Washington Times* (January 9, 2005), http://www.washtimes.com/metro/20050109-120804-4938r.htm.

19. "Pledge Father Seeks to Remove God from Money," *Associated Press* (November 18, 2005).

20. Ward, "Newdow Targets Use of Clergy."

21. "Ninth Circuit Court of Appeals Reorganization Act of 2001," http:// commdocs.house.gov/committees/judiciary/hju80880.000/hju80880_0.htm.

22. Hans S. Nichols, "Rulings from the Rogue Court . . ." *Insight on the News,* March 25, 2002, http://www.findarticles.com/p/articles/mi_m1571/ is_11_18/ai_84184980.

23. Fox News, *The O'Reilly Factor,* November 15, 2005.

24. "The Ninth Circuit Court Must Be Split," Traditional Values Coalition (http://traditionalvalues.org/pdf_files/NinthCircuitCourt04041.pdf).

25. "Ninth Circuit Rules Against Parental Rights," Traditional Values Coalition (undated online report: http://traditionalvalues.org/pdf_files/ NinthCircuitParentalRights.pdf).

26. Ibid.

27. Fox News, *The O'Reilly Factor,* November 15, 2005.

28. Robert Bork, "Our Judicial Oligarchy," *First Things* 67 (November 1996), 21–24, http://www.leaderu.com/ftissues/ft9611/articles/bork.html).

29. Mark Levin, *Men in Black* (Washington, DC: Regnery Publishing, 2005), 10.

30. Ibid., 53.

31. Robert Bork, *Coercing Virtue* (Washington, DC: The AEI Press, 2003), 8–9.

32. "Marbury v. Madison (1803)," Landmark Supreme Court Cases, Street Law & The Supreme Court Historical Society, http://www.landmarkcases .org/marbury/jefferson.html.

33. "President Jackson's Veto Message Regarding the Bank of the United States; July 10, 1832," The Avalon Project at Yale Law School, http://www.yale.edu/lawweb/avalon/presiden/veto/ajveto01.htm.

34. "First Inaugural Address of Abraham Lincoln," The Avalon Project at Yale Law School, http://www.yale.edu/lawweb/avalon/presiden/inaug/lincoln1.htm).

Chapter 8

1. Levin.

2. "Marbury v. Madison (1803)," Landmark Supreme Court Cases, Street Law & The Supreme Court Historical Society, http://www.landmarkcases .org/marbury/jefferson.html.

3. "A Constitutional Amendment Restoring Religious Freedom," Wall-Builders, http://www.wallbuilders.com/resources/search/detail.php?ResourceID =61.

4. Art Moore, "Punishment Includes Islam Indoctrination," WorldNet-Daily, October 31, 2002, http://*WorldNetDaily*.com/news/article.asp?ARTICLE_ID =29483.

5. "Swedish Minister Acquitted of Hate Speech Charges," *WorldNetDaily*, November 29, 2005, http://WorldNetDaily.com/news/article.asp?ARTICLE _ID=47633.

6. Robert Spencer, "Muslim Target," *FrontPageMagazine*, June 14, 2005, http://www.frontpagemag.com/Articles/ReadArticle.asp?ID=18349.

7. Bill Tammeus, "Attorney Renews His Fight against 'under God' in Allegiance Pledge," *Kansas City Star* (April 3, 2006), http://pewforum .org/news/display.php?NewsID=10292.

8. "House Votes to Bar Court Review of Pledge," *Associated Press*, September 24, 2004.

9. John Conyers' prepared statement on "Constitution Restoration Act of 2004," House Judiciary Subcommittee Hearing, http://commdocs.house.gov/committees/judiciary/hju95803.000/hju95803_0.htm.

10. Barry Lynn, "'Pledge Protection Act' Should Be Defeated in U.S. House, Says Americans United," Americans United for Separation of Church and State, press release, September 23, 2004, http://www.au.org/site/News2

?abbr=pr&page=NewsArticle&id=6903&security=1002&news_iv_ctrl=1358.

11. Quote from Representative Akin.

12. Susan Milligan, "House of Representatives Votes to Restrict Purview of Federal Courts," *Boston Globe* (September 24, 2004), http://www.highbeam .com/doc/1G1-122479220.html.

13. Rep. Todd Akin press release, "California-Atheist Michael Newdow Renews Assault On Pledge of Allegiance," http://www.house.gov/akin/ release/20050106.html.

14. Jim Abrams, "House Protects 'God' in Pledge," Associated Press, 9/24/2004: http://www.signonsandiego.com/uniontrib/20040924/news _1n24pledge.html.

15. Milligan, "House of Representatives Votes to Restrict Purview of Federal Courts."

16. "Public Expression of Religion Act of 2005," Library of Congress Thomas Database, http://thomas.loc.gov/cgi-bin/query/D?c109:2:./temp/ ~c109lFjECY.

17. Ron Strom, "Ex-ACLU attorney: Group 'terrorizing' U.S." World-NetDaily, December 28, 2005, http://WorldNetDaily.com/news/article.asp ?ARTICLE_ID=48098.

18. Ibid.

19. Bork, *Coercing Virtue*, 21.

20. "John Peter Muhlenberg," Institute on the Constitution, http://www .goconstitution.org/downloads/StudentNotebook.pdf, 118–19.